THE NARCISSIST'S LIFESTYLE

HOW TO LIVE AND DEAL WITH NARCISSISTIC PERSONALITIES

ALEXI HOOLEY

ALEXI HOOLEY

Copyright © 2024 by Alexi Hooley

All rights reserved.

No portion of this book may be reproduced in any form without written permission from the publisher or author, except as permitted by U.S. copyright law.

THE NARCISSIST'S LIFESTYLE

ALEXI HOOLEY

TABLE OF CONTENTS

Introduction 11

Chapter One 13

Why Be Concerned About Narcissism? 13
    Relationship Difficulties 21
    Violence at Schools 21
    Depression 22
    Other Personality Disorders 22
    Eating Disorder 22
    Physical Health Problems 23
    Drug and Alcohol Misuse 23
    Suicidal Thoughts 24

Chapter Two 25

The Science of Narcissism 25
    Where did the word "Narcissism" come from? 26
    Scientific Definition of Narcissism 27
    The Difference Between Narcissistic Traits and NPD 30
    The Origin Story of all Narcissists 31
        The Spoiled Child 34
        The Dependent Child 34
        The Lonely Deprived Child 35
        The Mixed Bag 35

Chapter Three 37

Understanding Your Narcissist - Schema Therapy 37
    The 18 Maladaptive Schemas 40
        Abandonment 40
        Mistrust 41
        Emotional Deprivation 41
        Defectiveness 41
        Social Isolation 42
        Dependence 42
        Vulnerability 43
        Enmeshment 43
        Unrelenting Standards 44
        Failure 44
        Entitlement 45

    Lack of Self-Control 45
    Subjugation 46
    Self Sacrifice 46
    Approval Seeking 47
    Pessimism 47
    Emotional Inhibition 47
    Grandiose 48
  How Schemas Create Narcissistic Traits **49**
    Emotional Deprivation 49
    Mistrust 50
    Defectiveness 51
    Subjugation 52
    Unrelenting Standards 53
    Entitlement 54
    Approval Seeking 55

Chapter Four 57

Types of Narcissists 57
  Core Elements of Narcissism **60**
  Sense of Grandiose **60**
  High Sense of Entitlement **62**
  Chronic Need for Admiration **63**
  Lack of Regard for Others **65**
  Types of Narcissism **66**
    Overt Narcissism 66
    Covert Narcissism 67
    Antagonistic Narcissism 67
    Communal Narcissism 67
    Malignant Narcissism 68
  Myths About Narcissists **68**
    "All narcissists are charismatic" 69
    "Narcissism is bad" 71
    "All narcissists are violent" 72

Chapter Five 73

Difference Between Narcissism, Sociopathy, and Psychopathy 73
  So, What Is Personality Disorder? **74**
  Differences Between Sociopathy and Narcissism **75**
  Similarities Between Sociopathy and Narcissism **76**
  Psychopathy **76**

Chapter Six 79

Understanding Why You Are Drawn To Narcissists 79
The Burden of Responsibility 79
The Story of Echo 80
The Curse of Echo 81
The Mind of a Victim 82
The Schemas of a Victim 83
Self Sacrifice 83
Subjugation 85
Abandonment 86
Emotional Inhibition 87
How The Brain Works During A Threat 89

Chapter Seven 91

Healing Yourself, The Art Of Mindfulness 91
Identifying Your Schemas 91
Identifying Your Triggers 94
Analyzing Yourself 96
Changing Yourself via Mindfulness 97

Chapter Eight 103

How To Manage Yourself 103
The Single Factor That Determines if a Narcissist Will Change - Leverage 103
Managing Your Narcissist 104
Know Your Narcissist 104
Most Likely Triggers of Your Narcissist 106
Communicating With Your Narcissist 107
Remain Calm 108
Allay Their Fear/ Doubt/ Pain 108
Assure Them Your Action or Inaction Was Not Meant as an Attack 108
Let them see that You Are Ready to Communicate if They Are 109
Let them see that their action Hurts You and Has Consequences .. 109
Run For Dear Life 109
What Not To Do 110
Do Not Apologize 110
Do Not Attack 110
Do Not Try To Change Him 111

Chapter Nine **113**
Becoming A Healthy Narcissist **113**
   Self-love 113
   Build Healthy Relationships 115
   Be Purpose Driven 116
   Take Pride in Accomplishments 116
   Develop Empathy 116

Conclusion **119**
REFERENCES **121**

THE NARCISSIST'S LIFESTYLE

Introduction

The condition of not being able to feel any emotion has always intrigued me, and the first word I ever came upon to describe people who had this condition was "narcissist." My curiosity got the better of me, and I began to devour every piece of information I came across online on this thing called "narcissism." The more I read, the more confused I got. But I wasn't alone, as I came to realize a lot of people shared my curiosity. Unfortunately, it was hard to tell who answered our questions correctly. So, I decided to take the bull by the horns and do profound research on what narcissism is all about. And I was glad I did—because everything I knew about the topic was wrong. My research equipped me with the proper knowledge and made me reevaluate my understanding of the world. I got answers to long-held questions about the human mind. But more importantly, it birthed in me a compassion for victims of narcissists.

This book is written to provide as much accurate information about narcissism as possible to help the billions of people who are currently locked up in abusive relationships with their narcissists. Some people are unaware that among us live a set of individuals who, due to their genetics and childhood trauma, are programmed to treat people like doormats. These individuals are themselves a product of the cruelty that characterizes human nature.

My utmost desire is that this book will set you on a path to healing and living a full and healthy life.

ALEXI HOOLEY

Chapter One
Why Be Concerned About Narcissism?

Alexander the Great, Genghis Khan, and a few women make for some grand and amazing stories.

According to Man (2007,2004, p.10), Genghis Khan represents many things to different people. To Russia, Persia, and the West, he is a maniac who murdered millions in his countless bloodthirsty campaigns - his tactics cruel and his method evil. To his native homeland, Mongolia, he is called the father of the nation, and the Chinese revere him as the founder of a dynasty.

Where Hollywood would tell stories of men like these, presenting them in great cinematic expressions, the exact horror they unleashed on Earth in their time is something the modern man may never fathom. What incidents could have created a mind like Genghis Khan to contemplate feats so grandiose as conquering entire continents to form one of the greatest empires known to man? What childhood tragedy could have bore a hole so deep in the heart of one man that he chooses to ascend high above other men so he can be called a god? What is so charming and magnetic about men like Genghis Khan that they can convince millions to follow them into certain death and destruction to achieve his goal?

History is replete with men like Genghis Khan - Hitler, Stalin, Idi Amin, and several Caesars - who bent the will of many to their bidding. Some were hated and remain hated even to this day. Some were loved, and even though they died eons ago, they have become objects of honor. Ironically, some of these men's deeds remain a bone of contention among historians, scholars, and conspiracy theorists. Case in point is the many who believe the concentration camps of World War II never existed.

On one end, it makes for amazing historical recounts within well-air-conditioned lecture rooms or conference halls when discussing Earth's bloodiest war campaigns. However, if we were to be transported via time machines to see some of these events, many wouldn't believe the horrors they would witness. One minute, you are being entertained by Hitler. He is jovial as he strokes his dog. A couple of children surround him, and he amuses them with a joke or two. The next moment, he is a fire-breathing dragon, motivating hundreds of thousands of men to burn down the earth. You might find it hard to believe what you are witnessing. You might even deny what you behold.

Unfortunately, this denial is the very horse upon which all things evil ride. You see, many couldn't believe Genghis Khan's men would attack their village, kill all the men, and rape the women. And like us, the reality of what a narcissist can do to us if they are let loose is foreign until we are lying in our blood.

Ironically, it is also this denial that keeps people as victims. The ordinary mind cannot fathom the amount of evil others can do to it. So, it stays in a catatonic state after it has been attacked. Sadly, this shock is what makes victims keep quiet. And we do keep quiet, for we know nobody would believe us, at least not until they become victims themselves.
But, so far, I have spoken of greats, men who were at the

helm of political and economic power in the past. But do we also have people today, ordinary in every way, burdened with the demands of a 9 to 5 job and a boring life, who are capable of unspeakable evil? Of course, they exist. But do we also deny their deeds? Yes, we do, despite history screaming at our faces that among us are men capable of causing untold damage to mankind. It would seem as though we do not listen. However, unlike the days of the Khans and the Caesars, where these men could pick up an axe and begin slicing their way to their perceived divine status (although some do), many are equipped in suits and ties, wielding massive portfolios. Many are lords of industries and influencers on social media with hundreds of millions of followers. Many are democratically elected political figures. Many are also in middle management of big corporations. Some are entrepreneurs running small businesses, heads of schools 'PTAs, family men, and even the quiet teenager nursing great ambition to match her preception of herself.

These individuals do not kill their victims. But they lodge themselves in the minds of their victims as haunted memories. Their tools include manipulation, gaslighting, lying, and a host of other weapons of emotional and identity destruction. I am talking about individuals who would puncture your car's tires, preventing you from getting to that interview you've spent months preparing for. These predators work covertly and overtly, and their victims live in denial of the fact that they are in a relationship with a narcissist.

So, to answer the broad question, why be concerned about narcissism? The answer is obvious: you get to wake up from denial and realize that you might be in a relationship with a monster.

But I do not wish you take my word for it. To help jumpstart your epiphany, I will share a short story with you. The purpose of this story is to create a conviction within you that beyond Hollywood and the glamour of history books, narcissists are real, and you probably are or have been a victim of one. You probably have crossed paths with a few, but you never knew. Perhaps it is that boss you once had, who, despite all your efforts to please, set you back years in your career. You probably explained the incident away as your fault. You probably assumed company policy was behind his actions. But you will come to see that you had a narcissist for a boss.

Some of you will come to know why your lovers seem to have you eating from their palms. They make you feel like you are not enough and must strive to be a better person to deserve their kindness. Unfortunately, some of you would begin to understand why it seems as though nature gifted you a teen from hell—a child you love so much but who is bent on destroying your peace of mind for no apparent reason.

At the end of this chapter, your curiosity about narcissism will evolve into a full-blown concern. You will come to accept the world as it is: a complex system. If you ever thought that all of humanity would finally live in peace and harmony one day, with no conflicts, put your seat belt on as you are in for some rude awakening. It is possible, but the odds are against such brazen hope.

I would love to clarify that the stories shared in this book are fictional; however, they are inspired by the many verified stories available in the public domain.

Mr. and Mrs. Stones
The photographer was patient; he had to be. Getting this

contract was a big deal. When the magazine called him and stated without mincing words that his style of photography was needed for their next publication, he was left speechless. Yet nothing could prepare him for the greatest surprise of his career when he was told he would be photographing the Governor-elect, Mr. Stones.

He couldn't believe he was now standing in the gallant sitting room of the Stones with his team, setting up gadgets. Upon his arrival, he was informed the Stones would be out to see him shortly. He stood staring at the biggest wall art he had ever seen when he heard a familiar voice from behind him, a voice that had come to mean something to the city, as it flowed from the TVs of a thousand homes promising to fight crime, put more money into education, equip the police, and tax the rich. He turned around and was immediately enveloped by the presence of Mr. Stones. He looked taller in person, and his smile broader. Mr. Stones shook his hand, informing him that he had asked the magazine to hire him specifically. "I have always loved your work," Stones said, looking at him directly in the eyes, "it reflects my style of creativity." The photographer didn't know how to react. He never knew Mr. Stones was also an artist. But it surely felt good that his work was loved by a man as influential as Mr. Stones. A few minutes later, everything was set up, with the graceful Mrs. Stones seated next to her amazing husband, both taking directions from the photographer.

The lens zoomed in, and one can see Mrs. Stones smiling and sometimes shifting position several times. It made the work a bit harder for the photographer, but he didn't mind. However, nobody would ever guess what exactly was happening!
"You will ruin this shoot, you fat cow," Mr. Stones whispered from the side of his mouth to his wife. "I emphatically told you

to cut down on carbs, didn't I?" Mrs. Stones uneasily smiled as she tried to maintain her graceful posture. She didn't want to make the photographers work hard. A few moments later, Stones notices the color of his wife's toenails. He couldn't believe it! "Why are your toenails painted red? Are you some sort of stripper?" Stones asked. He continued, "I do the most. I work out seven days a week, despite my schedule; I have been on the campaign trail for the past six months, and still, I have the time to look my best. What excuse do you have for not looking your best?" he snickered. Tears welled up in Mrs. Stones' eyes. She had to get to the restroom, signaling the photographer who came closer. "I need to freshen up." As she stood, her husband held her hands rather gently and pulled her closer to him. "You are perfect," he said ever so quietly, but loud enough for the photographer to hear. Mrs. Stones smiled. She saw the kindness in his eyes. A part of her wanted to believe he meant it, another part was confused. "Thank you," she responded. And as she turned to go, Stones whispered, this time within only her earshot, "If only you did what I ask you to do, you would be a better version of yourself." She paused in her stride, looked back at him, this time the tears freely falling, and said as she had a million times in their three years of marriage, "I will try my best."

The mind of a narcissist is a complex thing. Mrs. Stones is stuck within a well-cast web. Everybody sees a strong man who truly loves his family and city, ready to lay down his life for their good! She sees something else, a man insatiable. Nothing she does is ever enough. He has her buttons and knows what to press for his pleasure. She is consistently on her toes, walking on eggshells! During the campaign, she was involved in an accident. Opening her eyes on the hospital bed, she first saw Stones holding a bouquet with that ever-charming smile. She felt grateful. There were a few of his high-profile friends in the room with him. He was gentle and kind. The moment they were left alone, he went into a short tirade about how he had to leave the campaign trail just to see her, and he wasn't sure what the effect would be on his already slim chances of winning. Of course, he bent to kiss her and promised to visit her as he had other things to attend to. Reaching the door, he slowed down, turned around, and said, "You only had one job, to support me, yet somehow of all the cars in this city to run into a fucking brick wall, it had to be yours."

Victims of narcissists are often left bewildered. Does he love me? Does she care? Or am I just an accessory?

When Luke heard his dad had died, he didn't feel anything at first. He had cut the man off in his mind. Every attempt to conjure up some father-son memory was impossible. He had nothing to miss. A few months after the burial, he came across the space of narcissism on Quora. Many of the stories he read of the victims coincided with his. So, he began to study narcissism. And for the first time, he came to understand his dad more. It was as though wool was pulled from his eyes. In his case, he was able to put things together about how his father came to be the kind of man he was. His dad did attempt to contact him before he died, but Luke wasn't open to being abused again. Sadly, James realized perhaps the dad had changed. For the first time, he began to cry, and his tears still flow to this day.

Many relationships are in peril today because many are ignorant of how the human mind works. Victims remain on a path of self-destruction, consistently finding themselves in the arms of abusers. Abusers are not aware of the effect of their actions on those they love. Some are lost causes, forever cursed to damage others, while some might see the light.

Statistically, reports place the percentage of people in the US with NPD (Narcissistic Personality Disorder) to be between 0.5% and 5% (Cleveland Clinic, 2023.) This percentage doesn't account for those with high narcissistic traits (You can have high narcissistic traits without being diagnosed with NPD. These are terms you will come to understand later in the book), and it is limited to just the US. However, this number is still threatening as it takes just one man to destroy nations. With enough motivation, one madman can convince an entire tribe to destroy other tribes. What is the possibility that these 5 percent make up more than 99 percent of powerful men in the US? Several experts agree that most of the world's notable leaders are narcissistic. So much for world peace! In America, popularity polls are a big deal among politicians. "What percentage of people love me?" a senator would ask. Ironically, it doesn't take much to gain the people's love. Be charismatic, show that you are a man of the people, look good, and be able to talk a big game, all of which are traits most narcissists have mastered.

Unlike any time in the history of man, today, narcissistic traits are being celebrated, and the tools for self-centered expression (mainly social media platforms) are abundant. Should you and I be worried? I think so, more than ever before. Many of the problems we see in modern society can be linked to narcissism.

Below are a few reasons why you should care about narcissism.

Relationship Difficulties

Relationships are the bedrock of every society, starting from the family and extending to the giant socio-economic and cultural structure we see around us today. If we get relationships right at the basic level, we could solve most of today's problems, including crime. Sadly, the divorce rate worldwide is steadily on the increase. Could this phenomenon be because many are marrying individuals incapable of being in a healthy romantic relationship? Where the divorce rate itself is a big problem, children are often hit the most during divorce. Unfortunately, children raised in single-parent homes are more prone to abuse and mental health issues. It is like a cycle of death: Marriages crumble because one or both people are a narcissist; the divorce affects the mental health of the children, with some growing up to become narcissists or victims. Parents need to understand that how they raise their children determines to a large extent if they will end up self-centered, attention seeking, manipulative, or emotionally healthy.

Violence at Schools

Shootings in schools have doubled over the past twenty years, according to Stanford (2022). Toxicity in the workplace is a major issue. Not all violent crimes are a result of NPD, but most chronic personality disorders all have elements of NPD. Hence, the parents' work pauses after their kids are dropped at school, and the teachers must take over. Like parents, teachers must be taught how to handle difficult students to build healthy children. Many today have become pillars of society thanks to teachers and others who are not their parents who stepped in to correct flaws in their upbringings.

Depression

The link between depression and narcissism is a fact; however, it has not been researched deeply, mainly because narcissism is seen more as a neurotic disturbance. Narcissistic depression is predominant among children (Dimitris, 2017), while among adults, many are unaware that they are beyond what they know about themselves. Past feelings of childhood trauma stored in the subconscious can be triggered by events of today, which often lead to depression. Victims are struggling to set themselves free but do not know how. Through the study of narcissism, we can begin to understand, at least at the basic level, how the brain works, how habits are formed, and the impact of trauma on a child's brain. Ironically, we all are often just a few books away from conquering depression and anxiety.

Other Personality Disorders

A quote from me you will come across several times in this book is that "a narcissist can be violent, but he is not violent because he is narcissistic." Violence in people is often an undertone of a more chronic personality disorder. However, every personality disorder has an element of high narcissistic traits. Understanding narcissism can be the pathway to understanding other disorders like sociopathy and psychopathy!

Eating Disorder

There are a few unhealthy habits that many battle with that are linked to childhood trauma. A colleague narrated to me how an overweight parent would force her daughter to eat to make sure the daughter never loses weight. The mother scorns any revolt by the poor child, mockingly asking them, "Do you think you are better than me?" Many children are raised in homes where body shaming is a culture. These are children who grow up with an obsession to attain unrealistic body goals while shaming anyone who isn't as fit as them. Others grow up to have an unhealthy relationship with food.

Physical Health Problems

Most health problems can be traced to issues in the mind. Studies have shown that a healthy mind will beat the same disease that might take the life of another person with an unhealthy mind. There are children born with certain medical conditions and, depending on the environment they grow up in, are either made to feel shame or encouraged to socialize. It is not uncommon for families to hide that one child who is considered sick from the public. The child is made to believe he is less. Whether or not they beat the condition becomes a significant problem in that child's life. Some narcissists have an unexplainable hatred for the weak. When investigated, you realize they were shamed as children for being weak. Others have become prone to certain diseases (real and unreal.) These are reasons why we need to learn how our actions and inactions affect those we love.

Drug and Alcohol Misuse

Several reports and publications explore Alexander the Great's relationship with alcohol. Many conclude he didn't depend on alcohol, but he would routinely engage in uncontrolled drinking bouts, in which he killed one of his close friends, Cleitus the Black. Some of Alexander's darkest moments involved alcohol. Today, many high-performing individuals struggle with one substance abuse or another - this is a common theme among high-performing individuals as well as ordinary individuals—however, narcissism and substance abuse run parallel to each other.

Suicidal Thoughts

The origin of the name "narcissism" is a story that features the death of the main character almost entirely by their own hands. As fascinating as the stories might be, they reflect what unmet and suppressed desires can cause. Many high-performing members of society smile on the outside but battle mental issues. The difference between a narcissist and his victim isn't much. One is lashing out; the other is suppressing his feelings; same coins, different sides, each heading to the same deadly destination, an assurance of mutual destruction.

Chapter Two
The Science of Narcissism

I must note that this chapter should not be taken as an academic paper. It is only essential that we establish academic boundaries to prevent skewed perceptions about narcissism. This chapter is written based on my understanding from reading books and academic papers. Information gathered is then regurgitated in the easiest way for you to understand. However, for the sake of a more scientific audience, I expect that you study the materials I have learned as provided in the reference list of the book.

Human nature is as old as man. Yet, we are light years away from fully understanding exactly how we work, especially the mind. Several ancient civilizations - Egypt, India, Greece, China, and Persia - showed interest in unraveling the mysteries of the mind. Psychology as a field of study is just a few centuries old.

The first scientist ever to use the term "Narcissus-like" was Havelock Ellis in 1898. However, Narcissism as a trait has been in existence as long as man has been in existence. Do you remember all the greats I mentioned in the previous chapter? Today, many and more of their type who either brought great peace or terror are suspected to be narcissists (and some are outright psychopaths). Below is a list of these men and the year they were born.

Alexandre the Great: 20 or 21 July 356 BC
Genghis Khan: 1162
Henry VIII: 28 June 1491

Pablo Picasso: 25 October 1881
Julius Caesar: July 12 or 13 in 100 BCE
Herod the Great: 72 BC
Vlad III Prince of Wallachia: 1431

The list above excludes the undetected thousands, probably hundreds of thousands to millions of other individuals with high narcissistic traits who put their families, loved ones, villages, and entire communities on siege before the first ever patient was diagnosed with narcissism.

The point to be made here is that narcissism as a phenomenon predates its scientific discovery and nomenclature. However, with the help of science, today, we can understand what narcissism is. With a little bit of study, just about anyone can spot a narcissist a mile away. Victims can unravel the complications of their relationship with their narcissist and free themselves. Imagine the number of horrors that could have been prevented hundreds of years ago if people had access to the information you are about to get in this chapter.

Where did the word "Narcissism" come from?

To answer this question, we must go back thousands of years, specifically 8 CE. The name originates from 'Metamorphoses (Book III),' a poem written by Ovid, a Roman Poet.

There was once a young man named Narcissus, born from the relation between a nymph and a river god. The river god had but one warning concerning Narcissus: he must never see his reflection. Indeed, Narcissus was a beautiful man, and all who saw him wanted him. Unfortunately, he wanted nobody.

However, of all the people he rejected, there was a nymph named Echo, who took it the hardest as she was madly in love with him. Narcissus' rejection of Echo angered the gods, who cursed him. One day, as Narcissus wandered about, he saw a stream, and being thirsty, he knelt to cup a drink, and that was when he saw his reflection. He couldn't resist the beauty of the person staring back at him from the waters. He yearned to have this person so badly, but he couldn't. He cursed and prayed to the gods, but nothing happened. Sadly, Narcissus died, not knowing he was staring at his reflection.

An interesting story, wouldn't you agree? However, there are several versions of this story.

Some claim it was an evil spirit that tricked Narcissus into falling in love with his reflection. Another version of the myth is that Narcissus had a twin sister he loved deeply, who died! Upon seeing his reflection, he thought he was staring at his twin sister and yearned for her to return.

Irrespective of how the story is told, the fundamental theme remains. Narcissus was so madly in love with his reflection, something that wasn't real, and he died trying to get it!

A pretty sad story if you ask me.

Scientific Definition of Narcissism

The early definitions of narcissism centered around sexual love for one's self. Based on the story of Narcissus, Ellis (1898) termed the phrase "Narcisus-like" to describe the condition of "auto-erotism" (which means taking one's self as a sexual object) as observed in one of his patients. The second notable referral to Narcissus was by Freud (1905/1953, p.135-243), who used the terms ego-libido and narcissistic-libido to mean the same thing (self-love) in his publication, *Three Essays on the Theory of Sexuality*. However, both explanations aren't a part of how narcissism is defined clinically today.

It took a couple of years before narcissism began to be viewed as a form of personality when it was described as the God complex - a sense of superiority, aloofness, overconfidence, a strong need for praise, etc., by Jones (1913/1951). This work was followed by a more expansive theory on the root cause of narcissism. According to Freud (1914/1991), narcissism can be traced to the developmental phase of every child where it is required. He hypothesized that all children go through a stage of primary narcissism before they can also invest their "libidinal energy" into others. However, Freud believed this libidinal energy is limited, and there is just enough that a child can give out, and as such, it must be retained by receiving care and love from others, too. However, if by some form of parental negligence, care and love are not invested in a child, it will grow up compensating for this by focusing all its energy into loving itself – which practically is what narcissism is.

The first case of narcissism was published by Wälder (1925), where said patient showed extreme narcissistic traits, including over-confidence, superiority, a sense of extreme uniqueness, lack of empathy, maximum independence from others, and being overly logical. Other notable works on narcissism include that of Reich (1933), where light is shone on the sadistic nature of the narcissist - if they were to be ego-threatened, they could become offensive. It was also he who first linked narcissism to masculinity. Horney (1939) built upon the work of Freud, where she postulated that a narcissist's love for himself is built on qualities they do not possess, and as such, they are deluded, which is often linked to them not being loved properly as kids and as such their primary narcissistic traits developed into secondary narcissistic traits.

Throughout the twenties, a handful of notable scientists weighed in on narcissism as a personality disorder, some contradicting early work and others supporting them. However, it was the work of Otto Kernberg that was used to create the diagnostic criteria for Narcissistic Personality Disorder in the DSM-III. He defined narcissism as a form of borderline personality disorder and listed specific behaviors that can be used to diagnose pathological narcissistic personality (Kernberg, 1975).

Today, patients must have at least five of the nine criteria listed in the Diagnostic and Statistical Manual of Mental Disorders, 5th Edition: DSM-5.

- Grandiose sense of self.
- Preoccupied with fantasies of unlimited success, power, brilliance, beauty, or ideal love.
- Believes that he or she is "special" and unique and can only be understood by, or should associate with, other special or high-status people (or institutions).
- Requires excessive admiration.
- Sense of entitlement, unreasonable expectations of favorable treatment, or full compliance with his or her expectations.
- Exploitative, takes advantage of others to achieve his or her ends.
- Lacks empathy: unable to recognize or identify with the feelings and needs of others.
- Envious of others or believes that others are envious of

him or her.
- Shows arrogant, haughty behaviors or attitudes. (American Psychiatric Association, 2022).

The Difference Between Narcissistic Traits and NPD

I must emphasize that narcissism is a spectrum. Although Kernberg's work is fundamental to how NPD is diagnosed today, he did not support the continuous view of narcissism.

Narcissism today is defined as a spectrum, one end being what many call the healthy narcissist and the other being NPD. A healthy narcissist believes in himself and his capability, but his belief is based on fact. However, along the spectrum are high narcissistic traits that are dangerous. The extent to which these traits interfere in a person's life and the number of these traits determines exactly how narcissistic a person is.

To help you understand, consider someone; let's call him Mike. Mike is a highly competitive guy. He believes he is the best at his work and that nobody can get to his level. He boasts about it as much as he can. However, Mike's behaviour is unique to the workplace. He is a nice guy when he is not working. Also, if you call Mike out on his behaviour, he seems to understand but he just can't help himself.

Mike has a narcissistic trait of self grandiose at work, which can make him a douchebag sometimes, but he is not a narcissist.

Now compare Mike to Ross, his boss. Ross carries on with his grandiosity in every aspect of his life. He has no inhibitions to his beliefs and thinks he is unique, evidenced by how much he wants to be praised for doing regular stuff. Ross is exploitative, never sharing the limelight with anybody when things work well, and is quick to throw people under the bus when things do not work out. He carries on like he doesn't need a team and believes his team makes him slow. He is what is at work, at home, and at the club that he's been a member of for barely two months.

Ross is a narcissist.

The Origin Story of all Narcissists

We have established the fact that the interest in narcissism predates scientific research. We have also walked through the timeline of several scientific reports on this phenomenon. However, the one question and its other variants that require answering is, "How does someone develop narcissistic traits? Is it a virus like the flu? Or is it a learned behavior?"

Despite the several schools of thought on narcissism, a consensus is that narcissistic traits are developed from birth!

Every child is born with adaptive narcissistic traits! The world must revolve around them if they grow up to become healthy adults. A baby wants what it wants, and it must be made available. It doesn't care nor give a thought to the person who provides what it wants. A baby always gets what it wants! This is called primary narcissism, and it is required and fundamental to a baby's growth!

Imagine if babies were born with the intuition to know how their mum feels. Imagine if they understood what sleep deprivation does to the human body. Imagine a baby that innately knows that mummy and daddy are too broke for the month to buy its food! If such a baby ever existed, it would keep quiet when hungry. It would keep quiet when it wakes up alone at odd hours of the night in need of a cuddle. It would keep quiet when it messes itself up. It would probably think, "Mummy is broke," and so rather suck it up than scream when it is ill. These are not characteristics of a baby. And because a baby lacks all these, it wails for all the attention and love needed to grow. A baby does not care! Much like Narcissus, a baby sees only one person in the world: itself. It stays looking at its reflection, unable to give love to anyone but itself. It has no sense of gratitude. It thinks everyone owes it something!

Freud's theories on narcissism explain this in detail. It gives us a pivotal understanding of the developmental process of a child and how narcissists come to be. Every child has a "libidinal" energy to invest in others. This energy is limited, however. It is expected that a child grows out of his primary narcissistic traits and begins to invest his libidinal energy into others. This act must also be reciprocated so the child doesn't run out of steam. However, unique to narcissists is that instead of investing that energy into others as children, they direct the love to themselves. What causes a child to aim all its love to itself is often environmental: the parent not giving the child unconditional love, withholding attention, etc. This is one way to view why a child might grow up to be narcissistic.

The healthy development of a child encourages the departure from primary narcissism. It is, therefore, an anomaly when a grown man or woman retains these primary narcissistic traits. In fact, you would come to understand soon that most narcissists are just big babies, and the best way to treat them is as you would a kid via proper communication and assurance with the hope that their inner child heals. Now, where a baby can only scream and throw fits of anger when it is not treated like an emperor, a grown person is equipped with the most toxic of habits to ensure it gets your attention, including verbal, emotional, and physical abuse. But, you see, unlike a baby with limited needs, narcissists are insatiable, much like Narcissus, who longed deeply for a reflection - something that does not exist - narcissists long for something another person cannot give them. What they want is a piece of themselves. But they don't know this. So they will burn through victims upon victims like you, never finding what they want.

There are several schools of thought as to what could have happened to a child in its formative years to turn him into a narcissist.

First, we have the theory developed by Otto Kernberg, the Austrian-American psychoanalyst and professor who theorized that narcissism is pathological. According to him, narcissism develops when kids are at a very young age and are denied care, love, and attention during their developmental processes. The denial of these needs results in negative emotions that eventually affect the natural developmental process of the mind, which manifest themselves as maladaptive narcissistic traits as they grow older.

A second explanation is that of Heinz Kohut, who was an Austrian-born American psychoanalyst. He postulates that when a child stops receiving the required attention needed to soothe its adaptive narcissistic traits, the child would be stuck with its childish way of expressing its desire for such attention. This explains the term "big baby" that I used in describing narcissism earlier in the chapter.

However, a more interesting perspective on how narcissism is formed in children is seen in Behary (2018), where she grouped narcissists into four categories:
- The Spoiled Child
- The Dependent Child
- The Lonely Deprived Child
- The Mixed Bag

The Spoiled Child

Quite self-explanatory, these are narcissists who come from a home where they are treated like emperors! As a child, this narcissist was indulged and given everything they desired. There were no boundaries, and there were no consequences for acting wrong. Sheltered from discomfort and inconvenience, the child grows up with an unjust perspective of how life is both to its eventual detriment and those around him.

The Dependent Child

This narcissist springs from a home where one or both parents actively ensure he or she does absolutely nothing. The parent handled basic chores and responsibilities on behalf of the child. This child grows up with little or no sense of duty. These are narcissists who believe others exist for their convenience. Unable to lift a finger to help themselves or make any major decisions, they grow up depending on others for almost everything.

The Lonely Deprived Child

Conditionally loved as a child, this narcissist has grown up to be completely self-dependent and repulsive to help. He is also competitive and has extremely high standards for himself and those around him. As a child, he had one parent or two who was hard to please. The level of attention, love, and care he gets depends on his performance. This child was consistently criticized by his parents, with the hope that he would turn out well. The lonely, deprived child must take piano lessons, do more chores than needed, and finish up academic work on his birthday just to have his cake. Often, his parents live vicariously through this child, hoping he gets into a school like Harvard or becomes a world-renowned sportsperson simply because they couldn't achieve the same feat.

The Mixed Bag

Some narcissists are formed from a combination of two or more of the three origins mentioned above. These include:
- The Spoiled Dependent
- The Deprived Dependent

These types of narcissists are more common primarily because no human is influenced by one factor. We are complicated beings, a product of several environmental factors.

The spoiled, dependent narcissist is a horror. He or she believes they deserve the best of all things, yet feels a keen sense of shame for his/her inability to make the right decisions on how to get what they want. So, he covers the shame of being dependent by attacking those who criticize him. These are bosses in the offices who got there probably by strings pulled by their parents. They cannot perform minor tasks and know they need help. However, they are quick to fire people and malign anyone who criticizes or judges them.

The deprived dependent is the high-maintenance narcissist. Unlike the deprived narcissist, who is highly functional and tends towards perfectionism, the deprived dependent narcissist fears he can never meet up to the standard set by others no matter how hard he tries and also lacks the will to make key decisions. This narcissist is clingy to a fault. He is in constant need of assurance and holding of hands. He is less brutish compared to the other types of narcissists, but if forced to admit his failings, he might lash out.

These origins give us a sense of the background of most narcissists. But it doesn't yet satisfy our deepest curiosity: what are the inner workings of a narcissist? What happens in the brain during these childhood traumas, and are narcissists even aware of their actions?

To provide answers to these questions, I had to go deeper in my research of how the mind works and, more importantly, how the mind of a narcissist works. This led me to schema therapy. Everything I learned is discussed in the next chapter.

Chapter Three
Understanding Your Narcissist - Schema Therapy

Schema therapy is an integrative therapy invented by Jeffery Young. It is used in the treatment of personality disorders. Understanding schemas is key to understanding your narcissist.

Let us get our definitions right.

Temperament: This is the innate character of a child dictated by his DNA. This includes shyness, aggression, extroversion, buoyancy, etc.
Environment: A child specifically talks about its caregivers, early influence and people, and the dynamic of the relationship between the child and them.
Schema: Schema are fundamental beliefs of a child that come from the interaction of the child and its environment.
Adaptive schema: These are positive sets of beliefs a child has from his interaction with his environment.
Maladaptive schema: These are distorted beliefs a child has from his interaction with his environment.

Based on these definitions, let us look at how the mind of a narcissist comes to be.

When a child is born, it has emotional and physical needs that must be met if that child will ever grow up to be a healthy citizen. This child has a unique temperament, something defined primarily by its DNA. Certain temperaments of a child can change as it ages; however, how this happens isn't yet known. A child's personality will be determined by its interaction with the environment.

Using one of the origin stories, let me illustrate the power of temperament.

Two children are born to the same parents who are excessively demanding of them. They are both loved conditionally and are heavily criticized from a young age.

Child 1 goes on to be a very competitive, lonely, deprived child—a high-performing individual with notable accomplishments at a very young age.

Child 2 goes on to become a bum, unsure of his ability. He shies away from responsibilities. He has poor work ethic and doesn't care much about working hard.

Same environment: we have two children but different outcomes. The deciding factor could be the individual temperaments of the kids. Child 1 might be aggressive and adventurous and, if put under pressure, pushes back. Child 2 might be shy, timid, and drawn back under pressure.

What drives either of the children in the above is their schemas. As defined above, schemas are fundamental beliefs formed within a child's subconsciousness based on its interaction with its environment. The first child's exposure to criticism and being deprived of the required love and attention he rightfully needed as a child led to a fundamental belief that "nobody would love him unless he is the best at what he does." Unfortunately, this belief is negative. This explains why, growing into a young man, he would do anything to be the best. So, he ensures everybody around him sees all his awards and achievements. He is constantly talking about himself and putting other people down. He does this in a vain attempt to be loved. Everything he does is from a place of insecurity and fear that he isn't truly enough to be loved. That child yearning for its parent's unconditional attention is still very much alive. But he is ashamed of that child as much as his parents were, and he would do anything to cover that child up with accomplishment. Like Narcissus, this young man will forever be staring at that false image of a successful version of himself instead of staring deep at his soul and healing.

Unfortunately, this narcissist isn't even aware that he has this schema. This is because schemas do not exist in the logical part of the brain. A narcissist doesn't think, "I will be a narcissist today." His schema exists in the subconscious. What activates schemas are external conditions he faces daily. Consider the first child (let's call him Steve), who just got a job at an insurance company. On the first day, the boss arrives to address the new interns. In his speech, the boss refers to the fact that "high-performing interns" are celebrated in the firm. What happens immediately is that Steve begins to feel how he felt when he was a kid, and his dad told him he would get a birthday cake only if he topped his class. The emotion swells within him, activating his schema that nobody would love him unless he outperformed his competition. Then, Steve reacts according to his temperament, which is to go on the offensive side. So, he outshines everybody and makes sure everybody knows he did. He would use anybody to achieve the company's goal. No relationship is too dear to sacrifice on his way to the top.

In essence, everybody sees Steve, the star of the firm, who is also a douchebag. But Steve sees a man now worthy of love *because of his performance. He doesn't get the love but he gets plaques and awards. So he does more and more and more till he dies!*

What Steve has is called a maladaptive schema.

The above illustration explains how personality is formed. So, when you see a young woman who is driven and hard-working, you are witnessing the product of an interplay between her temperament and her environment when she was still a child.

The 18 Maladaptive Schemas

According to Young, Klosko & Wisher (2006), eighteen major maladaptive schemas exist. I have explained each schema with a short story for ease of understanding.

Abandonment

A narcissist with abandonment issues believes that loved ones will eventually leave, disappoint, or betray him.

Mary probably grew up in a household where either of the parents died when she was young. Other scenarios include one or both of her parents actually leaving and never coming back, being given up for adoption at an early age, betrayal of her trust multiple times, and breaking of promises made to her by her parents, who weren't around at major events in her life like dances, plays, graduations, etc.

Mistrust

A belief that nobody can and should be trusted no matter what.

Zlatan was sexually abused by a close relative who came to stay with them. He also witnessed the effect of one of his parents cheating on the other. Other scenarios might include the counselor at school telling other teachers about things Zlatan discussed with him, early childhood heartbreak from a crush, consistent disappointment by parents, and multiple broken promises by people he looked up to.

Emotional Deprivation

This is a belief that no one will ever be able to meet your emotional needs. These needs primarily consist of nurture, empathy, and protection.

Thai, at an early age, was often neglected. Perhaps his parents were consistently busy, working multiple jobs, or were invested in their careers, so he was left to be catered to by nannies. He didn't get the nurture a child requires from the mother. Because both parents were largely absent in his day-to-day life, they couldn't understand his daily struggles and so would respond to his requests brashly without empathy. After all, his parents reasoned, they put him in the best of schools. There was also no one Thai could run to for protection from bullies at school.

Defectiveness

Defectiveness is the belief that one cannot be loved because of obvious physical, mental, or behavioral traits.

Iris didn't begin to talk until she was about 4. And even then, she still found it hard to make full sentences until she was about 12. Her speech impediment was a major issue in her parent's relationship. She overheard her mother several times telling her friends that her dad had children with another woman for fear of them giving birth to another child with problems. Iris rarely saw her dad, and even when he was around, he rarely acknowledged her. Other defects might include being considered ugly, short, etc.

Social Isolation

This is a belief that one is not good enough to mingle with others.

Lizzy grew up fighting several diseases all her life. A month hardly goes by without her being scheduled for an operation or the other. The toll of her medical expenses meant her parents practically stopped her from going out and playing with other kids. She was home-schooled. When they had guests, she would be ordered to her room. Her dad always told her she was too weak to mingle with others.

Dependence

The belief is that one cannot do anything, including everyday activities, without messing up.

Jason wasn't allowed to do anything as a child, thanks to his doting mum. His childhood is filled with Mum picking his outfit, choosing his friends, and deciding his favorite snacks, even as a teenager. Today, he runs a small company, all thanks to his best friend and partner. However, Jason spends a lot of money on staffing. He covers up his inadequacies by consistently surrounding himself with people he can put in charge of things and then unjustly fires them when things go wrong.

Vulnerability

This is the belief in imminent danger. The fear that something terrible might happen at any given time.

At age 5, Musa had witnessed two civil wars in his small hometown. Then, by age 7, a major earthquake occurred. His dad did everything to move his family to the US. Upon arrival, his mum became clinically depressed and took her own life. At barely 14 years old, Musa had seen enough tragedy to last a lifetime. Today, he has more phobias than he can count and has PTSD. Despite all these, he has managed to build a thriving business and even has an NGO named after his mum.

Enmeshment

Enmeshment is the belief that one has no unique identity and must rely on others. This is, in a way, similar to dependence.

Garreth has always been close to his grandfather, fondly referring to him as Didi. His grandfather had a strong personality rooted in Mormon tradition. Gareth grew up soaking up everything Didi told him. He grew up being indoctrinated. Because he was shielded from other points of view and was taught that being dogmatic was required to be accepted, Gareth grew to know what Didi had only taught him.

Unrelenting Standards

This is the belief that you must live by internalized, unrealistic high standards set by you. This often leads to perfectionism, setting up rigid rules for yourself, and being consistently occupied to achieve more.

Adam's parents are considered geniuses, having advanced degrees in their respective fields, and are trail-blazing in their careers. For as long as Adam could remember, much has been expected from him. Not minding his natural inclinations and tendencies, his parents needed him to excel, even in minor tasks. Sports weren't recreational, music wasn't for fun, and field trips were a competition.

Failure

If you have this schema, you believe it will always fail no matter what you do. You think you're not as smart, gifted, or as skilled as others.

Davon lives in the basement of his mum's house at 25. He dropped out of high school, isn't particularly good at anything, and spends most of his time playing games. As a child, he was shy and rarely took part in any competition. There were several instances where his mum compared him to other kids in the street unfavorably. "Davon, why can't you be like Troy and go play basketball?" When he asked for a bicycle at 12, his mum told him he was too weak compared to the other boys, an excuse she gave only because she didn't have the money. It wasn't that Davon's mum set out to make her child feel like a failure; however, her communication with him was poor.

Entitlement

The belief that you have a right to do and act as you please without respect for the rules that guide others because you are better than everybody. You demand to be treated differently and believe you must always get what you want.

Sean was born to an upper-class family. Spoiled from childhood, Sean always gets what he wants. If Sean doesn't like waffles, nobody eats waffles in the house. If Sean doesn't like a maid, that maid is fired. Sean came first in everything his parents did! One time, Sean demanded he wanted to drive his father's car at barely 13, without a license. His father allowed it, and even though Sean hit another vehicle, it was sorted out! Sean is a king, Sean is an emperor, and Sean is a god!

Lack of Self-Control

The belief that you lack the will and inner strength to stop bad habits.

Luke's great-grandfather was a drunk. Despite owning one of the first stores in his town, he couldn't stop drinking to mingle with his business. His grandfather was notorious for sleeping with anything that had a hole. He was well on his way to becoming a Sheriff, but he had one too many affairs with the wives of other powerful men in the city. His father dropped out of the dream team that won the city's first football trophy because of his anger and excessive outbursts. Luke was raised by both his grandfather and father. His mum left when he was younger. He does not abuse substances, but he has an unhealthy relationship with food and hates a lot of activities like waking up early and exercising. He showed early signs of athletics, but his inability to control himself nipped any chances of actual growth.

Subjugation

This is the belief that it is better to keep quiet, allowing a bully or threat to have his way to prevent being attacked or abused.

James' father was brutish, and he was prone to fits of anger that can quickly turn violent. His father hates it when he says something and people object. For the sake of peace in the home, James grew up watching his mum agree to everything the dad said. But this wasn't a reaction towards his dad alone; his mum hated confrontation and would rarely speak her mind on anything.

Self Sacrifice

Self-sacrifice by itself is needed to an extent. We cannot always put ourselves first. However, as a schema, it is the belief that meeting one's needs is shameful.

Gabby's family has always kept their doors open from an early age. If it was either a stray, a homeless person, or even a traveler, they were never alone. Sometimes, they had a surplus; more often than not, they didn't, yet it did not stop Gabby's family from giving and helping. There were nights she went to bed with an empty stomach. She would complain but was met with disdain for not thinking about others. This was the theme of her childhood.

Approval Seeking

The belief is that you need to go to extreme lengths to get people's approval. A lack of self-gratification, so you only feel good about yourself when others approve of you.

Anthony grew up in a family of six. He was number five. Getting the much-needed affirmation and celebration children need as they grow was hard. His elder siblings seemed to be doing so well that his little wins as a kid were nothing compared to their achievements. But sometimes, he would do something so big and beyond. Only then would the family even remember he exists.

Pessimism

This is the belief that nothing good ever comes out of anything. It's all dark and gloomy. You only see the shadow and never the light in any circumstance—the inability to see the good in any situation. You believe strongly that something horrible will always happen and anticipate it.

Horrible life experiences as a child can cause this. Gyno lost his mum as a child in an accident. Dad developed complications months later from the accident that impacted him. His best friend, his only friend, moved away, so he had to spend most of high school alone. With Gyno, it was always one problem to another as a child. He fell off his bike and broke his tooth! His pet tortoise was smashed by a car!

Emotional Inhibition

This is the belief that expressing emotion is a thing of shame.

It extends into believing that emotions are misleading, thereby dismissing it and focusing only on logic!

Aminah's dad served in the army, and her mum was Catholic. She grew up in a strict home. Her mum taught her that a woman who laughed too much was a prostitute. She learned early to sit up straight, dress never to attract attention, and keep a serious face to keep all the bad boys away. Her father taught her the importance of being rational. Every time something sad happened to her, and she cried, her father would explain how to solve the problem and dismiss all the rubbish emotions she had.

Grandiose

This is when you believe you are superior to others. You think you are better than most people, and only a select few are your equal. This belief is often based on false or exaggerated standards you measure yourself.

Mark lived on the rich side of the city alongside his two siblings and his parents. He witnessed how his parents treated their house staff like they were nothing. His elder sister's friends were quizzed thoroughly to know if they came from reputable families. His elder brother wasn't allowed to be with a girl he liked because the girl was from the other side of the state!

So, there we have them, the 18 maladaptive schemas.

How Schemas Create Narcissistic Traits

Schemas activate when an individual is placed in an environment similar to the one that birthed such schema. Upon the activation of such schema, the individual will react. This reaction is dependent on the individual's temperament. Therein lies the inner workings of a narcissist. An individual is deemed to have narcissistic traits based on his response to a schema. Out of the 18 schemas discussed, there are specific ones associated more with narcissism. I have listed these schemas below, as well as the reaction to these schemas that we call narcissistic traits.

Emotional Deprivation

A reaction to this schema might be to never be in a position where you need someone. The narcissistic traits here will be emotional unavailability and hyper-independence. This individual will also misread the intentions of people around her. This narcissist, even though she is seemingly independent, will keep her distance from her partner over minor issues like his decision to spend the holidays with his parents. Her victims would always feel as though they are not needed when they try to connect with her emotionally, yet be severely punished when they choose to give her space.

Consider Mary, who has this narcissistic trait. She rarely communicates her emotional needs, which leaves her husband consistently guessing. Her strong sense of independence attracted him to her in the first place. She seemed low maintenance at the time, which he found quite interesting. As the relationship aged, he soon realized he had bitten more than he could chew. She had the caustic habit of disappearing for days and even weeks without telling him. When she does show up, she accuses him of neglecting her and being emotionally unavailable. At first, he would react by being kind and offering her succor, love, and nurture when he observed she was emotionally down. But, she would shun his approaches and even scorn them. There are also many instances where she would act out in a disappointed and angry manner over irrelevant issues.

A typical scenario might be him informing her he might be coming late from work. She suddenly feels abandoned, like she felt when she was younger. This triggers her schema, to which she reacts by telling him he is insensitive for not knowing she needs him that day. When he then offers to call in sick, she tells him she doesn't need him and punishes him by blocking him on all social media platforms and deleting his number from her phone.

Mistrust

A reaction to this schema would be never to trust anybody, no matter how close or well meaning they may be. The narcissistic traits might include extreme jealousy, in which lovers are consistently being obsessively monitored; extreme demand for assurance from friends, acquaintances, and loved ones; perception of others as betrayals even where there is no evidence or past incidents to prove such betrayal; prejudice and hatred towards a particular race, sex, tribe, etc.

These narcissists' stories always make for amazing movies. The theme always borders on jealous boyfriends, obsessive husbands, and over-controlling partners. I have seen friends get burnt dealing with this type of narcissist. A lady falls in love with a charming young man. Everything seems okay until he starts acting weird. He quizzes her over every man he sees her talk to. He smashes things in anger when she receives calls from male colleagues at work when at home. He consistently excuses his obsession, calling it love, and showers her with flowers and gifts. She assures him he is the only one, and everything seems okay, but for just a few days. He calls her a slut and a cheat for smiling at a stranger on a date. Again, these stories are common to many Hollywood movies.

This narcissist is also weary of acquaintances, co-workers, or neighbors who are nice to him. He doesn't believe anybody deals with altruistic intentions. Mistrust is also the reason why you hear certain words like "all men are pigs." People who make statements that generalize a group of people as evil are often dealing with mistrust. This schema can be activated by simple things like looking a certain way, talking, or touching the narcissist in a certain way. Irrespective of how innocent your intentions are, he will react.

Defectiveness

A narcissist with this schema would react to situations that make him feel unloved by becoming obsessive with work. The goal for him is to distract his mind from the feeling of shame that comes with the schema. You can also expect this narcissist to react irrationally if he thinks he is being treated without care. His mind distorts the actions of others to him to be a verification of the fact that he is unlovable.

You can be sure to catch Jack in the office first thing in the morning, head buried deep under a lot of files, doing what an entire team should be doing. He rarely has time for small talk and probably has no friends. However, he cherishes moments when the head of the department or management portrays him as a model staff. One would take his straightforward lifestyle to mean simplicity. Unfortunately, his wife at home bears the brunt of Jack's narcissistic habits. The two years of marriage have worn her out completely. Jack is hypersensitive to criticism. Everything she says is always assumed to be an attack on his personality. He would make cutting remarks like, "Guess what, if you don't love me at home, they love me at work." He insists she makes no friends nor be close to her family again because, according to him, "all they do is talk about him." He is always quick to point out things he has done for her and considers her an ingrate for not reciprocating his love for her. Her attempt to be his loving wife is painted as a pretense.

Subjugation

This narcissist reacts to his schema by relinquishing his ideas and perspectives to an assumed authority figure. Then, turning around, he attempts to control others he has a degree of authority over.

The subjugate always seems like the model staff—the one who always has the boss's back. Everything the boss says is correct since he dreads confrontation. His biggest fear is being fired or attacked by anyone ahead of him. This is that narcissist who seems to have figured out what needs to be done on an issue at work and has informed his team members, all of whom have agreed to discuss it with management. However, at the slightest criticism of the idea by management, he throws both the idea and his colleagues under the bus to take a stand with the boss. Unfortunately, his loyalty is not altruistic, as he will be found heavily criticizing those ahead of him, yet he lacks the courage to speak his mind even when given the chance.

Ironically, this narcissist is vastly controlling of those below him. Everyone must abide by his rules. He can be seen shouting and barking orders at his PA, secretary, and interns. He gets his kick from making them feel dumb. This character bears a semblance to Louis in the Series SUITS. He lacks the courage to face Harvey or Jessica because of their status, but when given the chance, he stabs them in the back over and over.

Unrelenting Standards

This narcissist reacts to his schema by setting extremely high standards for himself whenever he feels challenged. You can almost see his eyes twerking at board meetings where his achievements are being compared relative to others. He always wants to be the best. He is that student who gets mad when he scores a 97 and the next person after him scores a 98! After all, he is the best, and nobody can beat him except himself!

This trait is usually observed in high-performing individuals across all fields. Competitiveness turns certain men into some sort of legend. I am talking about Michael Jordan, Lebron James, and Christiano Ronaldo. They out-train everybody by miles, out-prepare everybody by years, and turn themselves into dependable machines. However, if not well managed, they become ruthless and lack empathy toward others. They formulate stringent regulations and rules that have no bearing on their goals, but they live by these rules nonetheless. Some are terrible at teamwork and sometimes believe the team is drawing them back. They are a one-man team that is impossible to please and hard to emotionally connect, as they have no time for basic human needs; after all, they are gods.

They loved to be challenged. Don't tell them "something cannot be done," for that is all they need to prove you wrong. When they don't achieve a goal, they are devastated, feeling like failures. Their failure (which is greater than other's success) can drive them to bouts of depression.

Entitlement

This narcissist's schema is triggered when they are refused anything. They consider the word "NO" an insult to their divine existence, and they react in ways that would leave their victim emotionally crippled.

This is the blonde girl on the cheerleading team who always has her way. Her father is most likely the biggest donor to her school, so she feels like the rightful queen overall. She cannot be told "no!" She picks who to date, and the lucky champ must accept her. After all, she believes she is raising his social status. When refused, she calls down thunder in the name of her parents and promises to obliterate her victim from Earth. She is always surrounded by the many she has conquered, whom she uses as her slaves.

But this narcissist isn't always glamorous. You have the average-looking Joe who believes he is the epitome of masculinity, and he cannot take "no" for an answer. When he walks in, he stands to take in the admiration of all the females in the room. The one girl who doesn't acknowledge him must be made to bow before him. So he hatches plans to get her. The more she ignores his existence, the more sinister his plans become. Many like him are cooling their heels in maximum security prisons for doing insane things to their victims.

Other variants include the lazy snub who feeds off the hard work of those around them. These are the bums who wait patiently for the death of a loved one so they can inherit large fortunes. These greedy ones believe the world owes them something and never feel gratitude towards their benefactors.

Approval Seeking

This narcissist reacts to feelings of not being sufficient by going overboard to seek approval. When his deeds are not publicly appreciated, he becomes angry and spiteful.

The approval seekers are your show-offs. They are usually the loudest in a room, ready to show their over-the-top knowledge of discussed topics. There is only space for them and them alone, as they desperately need the applause and probably an encore. The approval seeker in a relationship is loquacious and unable to keep secrets. He tells you everything about everybody, and you can be sure your secrets are not safe with him as he would tattletale them to the next person. They are the masters at name-dropping. They embellish the truth and speak half-truths to gain people's attention. They feel you're disloyal when you speak about others to them and they always want to be the topic in your mouth.

ALEXI HOOLEY

Chapter Four
Types of Narcissists

Alan was sweet and charming. It was hard not to notice his smile, as it was as contagious as a smile could be. There was also a deliberateness to his every gesture. A man like him would sweep any lady off her feet, and he knew it, but he seemed humble about it.

I was at a place in my life where the only thing that counted much to me was my work. I had moved after my divorce. But it wasn't the divorce that solely motivated me. At worst, I could have moved in with my parents, but they made it obvious they wanted nothing to do with a child who had put her feelings first before the family's status. My ex was the son of a notable person, and I came from a family of high status. So, instead of staying around to be reminded covertly by my parents that I was self-centered, I moved away to a quieter town. It had enough activity to keep my consultancy business alive throughout the year. And where it lacked the sense of community unique to smaller towns, you could feel its people are amazing.

Standing in front of a large collection of business books in one of the city's major malls was where I met Alan.

We immediately struck up a friendship. But who was I deceiving? I knew I wanted him. And so, after a few weeks, we began to date. Everything seemed just fine. He was supportive, patient, and kind within the first two months. And that was when trouble began to brew.

It started with snide remarks he would make, implying I thought I was better than him. Of course, I was better financially, but it never crossed my mind we competed as he seemed to be doing well himself. When I confronted him about his statements, he would shrug it off, telling me I was imagining things and that he would never imply such. I began to slowly doubt myself. These covert attacks continued for several months. He targeted my look, my work ethic, and my choice of friends.

After six months, the biggest revelation of the relationship came up. Alan was a divorcee with two children. One was 17 going on 18, and the second was 22. Both were boys. I only got to know thanks to my secretary, whose kid attended the same school as his kids.

This came as a shock. I confronted Alan again, to which he calmly responded that he had informed me on our first meeting. I was certain he didn't. I accepted and told him I would love to meet his kids. I shouldn't have. We decided to go on a joint vacation, all four of us.

For the first time in my life, I experienced manipulation beyond my understanding. John, the younger son, seemed quiet. He, however, was as difficult as a teenage boy can be and worse. John wasn't doing well at school. Everything he demanded must be given to him. When his father turned down his request, he would rant about how he never wanted to be a part of "this stupid trip." Twice, he approached me behind his father's back for some cash. Of course, I refused, and both times, he told me I could never replace his mom in his father's life.

Alan's first son, Perry, seemed more like the father in looks and charisma. The first time he saw me, he complimented me rather kindly about my looks. Then he directed the conversation to how much he appreciates beautiful women and how his current girlfriend is, in fact, a bombshell. Then he laughed awkwardly, leaned forward, and whispered how he had probably ten more of her type he was currently dating. I smiled back at him nervously. At every moment we were alone during the trip, he had something boastful to talk about! I couldn't be rude, so I just listened and acted surprised and amused on cue- he seemed to like that a lot. Alan, on the other hand, seemed to enjoy Perry's rabbling. One time, he turned to look at me, and with pride in his eyes, he announced how much he looked like him. It felt cringe. John didn't like that the father seemed more pleased with Perry than himself. He would attack Perry mid-statement, criticizing his need to talk about his achievement all the time, to which Perry would respond by listing a couple of John's failures. Once, John stood up and left the table, only to emerge a few seconds later asking for his father's car keys! It was chaotic.

At the end of the trip, I could bet neither of the children knew anything about me. Probably the only thing they would remember was that "I thought I was something," as the father put it. He seemed to have said it as a joke, referring to my business and busy schedule. I felt embarrassed. But it wasn't something new. I had a thick skin and self-confidence. I knew then that I wanted nothing to do with this family. Immediately returning to the city, I broke things off with Alan!

In the story above, we see three different characters. Each one is quite troubling yet unique. The question is, which of them is a narcissist?

Alan is a master at gaslighting. He is also competitive, as seen by his unease with his girlfriend, who is richer and more influential than him. He is, of course, charming, but he hides his insecurity well enough! Then we have the spoiled 17-year-old son. He has nothing much to boast about in terms of academics, and he lacks the grace his father possesses. He is critical and uses words as a weapon when he doesn't get what he wants. Then we have Alan's first child, who might be nice but is very boastful and is always seeking praise!

Based on the three personalities, we will look at some core elements of narcissism and the types of narcissists that exist.

Core Elements of Narcissism

There are four elements of narcissism. Each of these elements is a result of a combination of several schemas. Many publications refer to these four elements as also the four foundations of narcissism. They include:
- Sense of grandiose
- High sense of entitlement
- Chronic need for admiration
- Lack of regard for others

Let's look at these elements one after the other.

Sense of Grandiose

A high sense of grandiosity is sometimes confused with high self-esteem. Both are different. In psychology, grandiosity is a sense of superiority and uniqueness. It is the belief that one is better than others.

On the other hand, high self-esteem is believing in one's ability to the point where they are convinced they are equal to others. Someone with high self-esteem would say, "If others can do it, so can I." A person with a sense of grandiosity believes they are better than everybody!

However, I must state that there are certain instances where it is clear we are better than some people in certain tasks. Perhaps we are gifted (dance, sports, physics, calculations). So, within context, a grand master chess player might say, "I am one of the most gifted players in the world." You would notice that the conversation is about a certain skill, not the human experience's wider context.

Grandiosity in a narcissist, however, puts all humans below him. His sense of superiority is supreme and is often based on false proof and belief! Another way to view grandiosity is to imagine someone who believes others are below them. Someone with a sense of grandiosity would do any of the following:

- Consistently talk and boast about his accomplishments, whether true or not!
- Consider themselves more talented and gifted than others.
- Cannot stand others winning and so dismiss the achievements of others.
- Has no sense of teamwork, nor is ever ready to share the glory of an achievement.
- He believes with or without others, he can achieve whatever he sets his mind to.
- Because of his sense of self, he thinks he is above the rules that govern everybody.
- Hates all forms of criticism and never wants to be

corrected.
- Reacts offensively when corrected.

High Sense of Entitlement

This narcissist was raised by parents who did everything for him, gave him everything he wanted, and treated him like some sort of deity. This person grew up getting everything he wanted, anytime he wanted it. He probably was also shielded from the realities of life. When he broke his bike, it was replaced immediately. He got a car for his 14th birthday, one he crashed a few weeks later, and he got no rebuttal for it. This child grew up believing everything and everyone is for his divine pleasure.

But this high sense of entitlement isn't peculiar to kids raised in wealthy homes. Children show displeasure when they don't get what they want. From screaming at midnight when they're hungry to stomping their feet in anger when they don't get the toy they wanted on their sixth birthday. The question is: did either of the parents react with positive reinforcement to correct some of these reactions? Simply leaving a child to express anger and frustration when he doesn't get what he wants without letting the child see that life does not work that way will leave the child thinking his reactions are justified.

This sense of entitlement is seen in John in the opening story of this chapter. Perhaps being the last son, the father probably gave him everything he wanted. Any form of positive reinforcement only began when he had become a teenager, and it was sparse. So, despite flunking in school and being less than an average student, this young man, who's 17, believes he deserves all he asks for. And if he is refused, he reacts with emotional and verbal abuse. We all have met people like these who cannot take "no" for an answer. They believe they deserve all they want. Ironically, the more you indulge them, the more they demand. And when you reject them, they throw out everything you have ever done for them at your face.

Chronic Need for Admiration

A chronic need for admiration can sometimes be confused with a sense of grandiosity. This is because both traits share certain symptoms, primarily boastfulness. But where they differ is that a narcissist plagued with a sense of grandiosity doesn't need your admiration. He lives in an alternative world where he is the numero uno, and he is simply telling you (boasting). However, where a narcissist with a chronic need for admiration also believes he is better than everyone, he wants you and everyone to sing his praise. In his world, he sits on a throne high above everyone, somewhat like a God, and feeds off the worship of those around him.

Babies are adorable. Adore means to be fascinated by something so much that you give it special treatment. To adore is almost likened to worship. A really cute baby gets its praise sung everywhere it goes.

Oh, she is so cute!
He is beautiful!
Look at that smile!
And on and on!

Again, all of these are needed if a baby grows into a healthy member of society with high self-esteem. However, when this adoration is taken out of proportion to a point where everything the child does, from either pooing or existing, is met with unnecessary glee and celebration, a monster is being made. The child begins to assume he is some sort of demi-god! Every single thing he does, he begins to expect praises to be sung on him. This is how terrors are born. This is how dictators are formed.

Fortunately, not everybody is born into a mega-powerful family backed by an entire nation's military to force millions of people to worship us. Most of us are just regular folks. And even the ultra-wealthy among us have a limit to how much they can buy adoration from people. The narcissist in this scenario then resorts to outlandish boasting. He will say anything, do anything, and act in any way to purchase brief moments of awe from people around him. This is the case of Alan's first son, who seemed hungry for admiration. He wanted to hear at every instance how great he was, how attractive he was, and what a pleasure it was for anyone standing before him.

Sadly, this narcissistic trait isn't unique to men, who, as children, were heaped with too much praise. It is also peculiar to people who grew up in households where positive feedback is metered out to children only based on their performance. As mentioned earlier, every child requires an abundant dose of praise as a baby. However, this praise must be reduced to realistic standards. But more importantly, a child must never be shown love, care, and attention based on what he can and cannot do. Every child must feel secure that no matter what, they are accepted. This is the foundation upon which discipline works. Once a child is made to believe that he must act in certain ways before being appreciated, he will grow up with a chronic need for admiration. These are men and women who talk only about themselves, exaggerating truths and pushing false narratives about how great and important they are. They are quick to tell you how many countries they have traveled to, how many languages they speak, the number of women they slept with, and more and more without ever stopping.

Lack of Regard for Others

The fourth and the most damning element of a narcissist is their almost lack of empathy. In the expose on Freud's theory on the formative years of a child, we see that a narcissist at an early age would revert to "self-love" if he were denied the attention and love it requires to grow into a healthy adult. Your narcissist is capable of empathy, but sadly, he/she lives in a world where the only person who deserves love is himself.

Fundamentally, you must understand this fact about narcissists. Many lovers, parents, and good people struggle with it. Many misread the initial attention they get from a narcissist as love. However, in most cases, when a narcissist goes overboard to do anything nice, it is often for self-soothing purposes. So, take a narcissist with a sense of grandiosity, for example. Such will make a big entrance, showering you with gifts and attention so you can look up to him in his majesty. His intentions are flawed but masked. You draw close to such, believing this person loves you, only to be trapped in a cycle of mental abuse. You get treated with disgust. You wonder, "Why doesn't this person just leave me if he doesn't care?" All the while, your narcissist does not see you but himself. He cares for only himself. How can he give love when, as a child, he wasn't given love?

Unfortunately, these kinds of people are at the head of most organizations and, more specifically, at the helm of government affairs. The term "politics is a dirty game" fits perfectly. If men with normal-sized egos and reasonable empathy for people were in charge, maybe the world would be a better place. But that isn't the case. Third-world countries are plagued with leaders who would grab onto power for as long as they can. They make grand entrances like the Messiah their people need. Charismatic and armed with tongues that can set the world on fire, they sway the emotions of the masses to themselves, eliminating old regimes. Sooner than later, their greed for all the air in the world to fill up the emptiness in their lungs turns them into the very beasts they trampled on to become leaders! So, can a narcissist feel empathy? Yes! But more for themselves than for others.

Types of Narcissism

There are five types of narcissism.
- Overt Narcissism
- Covert Narcissism
- Antagonistic Narcissism
- Communal Narcissism
- Malignant Narcissism

Overt Narcissism

Overt narcissism is characterized by charm, a sense of grandiosity, pride, and over-confidence. Overt narcissists appear to be larger than life and attract much attention to themselves with their ability to sway the crowd in their favor. They are the heads of organizations, movements, and political leaders. They curry favor with other powerful people. An overt narcissist can be a man or a woman. Their true nature is often hidden from the public until tales of their nastiness start leaking, usually from those closest to them.

Covert Narcissism

Covert narcissism also includes the mindset of being better than others; however, a covert narcissist isn't flamboyant, popular, or necessarily successful. Covert narcissists are critical and abusive and are masters of gaslighting. They lack the social grace and influence of the overt narcissist but, if well placed, can cause major damage in any system through cunning and indirect attacks in an attempt to draw attention to themselves.

Antagonistic Narcissism

Antagonistic narcissist is obsessed with competition. These would do anything to consistently come out on top. Yes, they also have a sense of superiority over others, but they get their kick from putting others down. It is never a fair game with an antagonistic narcissist, and they fight with gloves off and dirty. They don't just want to feel superior; they want you to say it with their legs on your neck!

Communal Narcissism

Communal narcissism features self-sacrificing traits. These narcissists believe they are morally upright and generally better people. They latch on to community services and make sure everybody knows. They often have righteous rages on both insignificant and significant societal issues. They are masters of virtue signaling and are always ready to jump on new causes.

Malignant Narcissism

This is the worst form of narcissism and is associated with those diagnosed with NPD. It is an extreme personality disorder with the same sense of superiority but expressed in violence. This narcissist shares traits similar to antisocial disorder. He is dangerous to others as well as to himself.

Myths About Narcissists

In writing this book, great effort was put in to ensure every word remains within the boundary of the great work done so far by professionals and the science community on the topic of narcissism. And, if you were patient enough to read through the last chapter, you probably know more about narcissism than 99 percent of most people. However, as with any phenomenon that intrigues, there will always be an excess of information, mostly unverified, and narcissism is not spared. Before I began writing, all I knew about narcissism I read directly from Quora. And oh, was I misled.

So, I have taken the liberty to compile myths (wrong perspectives) about narcissism and then provide context to some while completely trashing others. Consider this chapter icing on the cake of the previous chapter.

"All narcissists are charismatic"

You walk into your living room, and you can already perceive the smell of alcohol. It is barely 7 am! Sprawled on the sofa dabbed in a robe is your husband (it could be your 25-year-old son, who begged to spend the night again at your place, or your cousin. It doesn't matter). He holds the remote to the TV in one hand as he leisurely swirls the contents of a beer bottle with his other hand. There is a certain haughtiness to him, a sense of self-importance; however, you do not see it. All you see is a "piece of shit" you can hardly bear. But your perception doesn't matter anyway.

He hears your footsteps but ignores you nonetheless. You walk towards your kitchen. And just as expected, you hear him babble something. You have learned to always listen up when he speaks to prevent the usual snark remarks he shoots at you for having him repeat himself. You could make out a few words from the nonsense he spewed, something about "great people wake up early." You feel the need to tell him you had worked into the night, studying for some presentation at your workplace, but you decide not to. A few seconds later, you hear him bark an order: "Make me some toast, would you?" Of course, you made him his toast.

As you take the toast to him, you observe him from the back. He lacks charisma and isn't particularly good-looking. He is not "the man," something you know from watching his reaction whenever he is near people who are better than him. He reacts to their every gesture with calculated reactions, laughing at jokes that are not there, barely looking at them in the face when he speaks.

Still, somehow, you seem to be the only one he has wrapped around his fingers. You know you could do better. But, still, you stay. YOU STAY!

But, even as you read this story, you refuse to see the patterns and accept the fact that what you are dealing with is a narcissist. "He cannot be," says your rational, "he lacks charisma, nor anything worthy of pride," says your reasoning.

But guess what?

All narcissists are not charismatic! Unlike the head of your department in the office who is a winner, is in great shape, drives a BMW, and makes sure he reminds everybody he is a graduate of Harvard (among other amazing things about himself), the piece of work sitting on your furniture has absolutely nothing to be proud of.

A narcissist doesn't need to be glamorous or be a high achiever. Your narcissist, probably at a young age, was subjected to verbal abuse where he was told he was nothing. Let us imagine he had a drunk for a father and a mother who worked three jobs and was rarely available. He was deprived of the encouragement and mental support every child needs to face the many struggles of life. Today, he is still that kid locked in a grown man's body. To cover up the shame he has for himself, he creates false narratives to make himself feel important. He shows false humility to people he assumes are well ahead of him. He sees what he thinks he is, but he isn't. So he forces some camaraderie, as seen by his awkward reactions to them. He begins to attack their personality when they draw near. He needs the verbal assurance that he, too, is "important." Unfortunately, much like Narcissus, the image he has created of himself does not exist.

As you walk out the door that morning to be a value-adding citizen of the world, you're below average looking, alcoholic, and painfully hard-to-live-with partner remains sprawled, probably asleep. Another big baby who will wait till you return to suck your life force so he can feel better. But he will never get better, even though you hope so, not unless he takes his eyes off the false reflection of himself and instead feeds himself with the truth that "he is enough."

"Narcissism is bad"

Before researching this interesting topic about narcissism, I ordinarily imagined narcissists as charming individuals who seduce both men and women, gain their trust, and then drag them to their basement to torture them to death! Several movies like Hanibal reinforced these definitions in my head! But I was wrong. Ironically, after my research, I came to see narcissists as the popular girl in school with three friends she uses to feel better and with whom they consistently bully the "new girl."

Now, we have already established that we were all born with primary narcissistic traits, which are required for survival as babies. Some of these traits remain even as we grow. However, it is expected that we learn to balance our self-centeredness with benevolence via proper training and exposure. In essence, we still need to retain some narcissistic traits into our adulthood.

You need a healthy dosage of self-belief, a little bit of that self-love, to be a high-functioning individual. You need to love your voice and be comfortable in your skin. However, we must not go over and beyond to assume we are better than anybody or in competition with anybody. We also must be realistic with our estimations of ourselves. You are not perfect, and nobody is. However, our imperfections are nothing to be ashamed of!

You do not need to look like Brad Pitt to "feel" you are good-looking. Brad Pitt is more handsome than most, but that alone isn't what makes him lovable. The same goes for you; there is something about you that is also amazing compared to others, including Brad Pitt! Nobody is better than the other. This is healthy narcissism.

"All narcissists are violent"

The best way to explain this is that a narcissist can be violent, but he is not violent because he is narcissistic. Violence is a symptom of a more dangerous personality disorder like psychopathy.

So, no, all narcissists are not violent. Extremely violent people most often cannot feel emotions for others. However, a narcissist does have the capacity to feel, but they are more in tune with their own needs. A narcissist is like a wounded animal; any attempt to cuddle, and they will try to bite you. Unfortunately, most narcissists are even unaware they are damaged. But there is hope, as injuries can be taken care of. With proper treatment, a narcissist can be nurtured back to help.

Chapter Five

Difference Between Narcissism, Sociopathy, and Psychopathy

If you have paid attention to aspects of this book where I encouraged self-diagnosis as a victim, as well as in diagnosing your narcissist, you would notice I encourage visiting a professional as the most sensible thing to do. In this chapter, you will come to understand why that is. In the broad topic of personality disorder, there are so many aspects to consider, so much that, to the informed, a disorder is often mistaken as another. Worse, certain conditions are not recognized as personality disorders yet have gained popularity, so much so that movies have been made about them. No personality disorders have been misconstrued, mistaken for each other, or wrongly represented as narcissism, sociopathy, or psychopathy.

However, before you can fully understand these individual concepts (narcissism, psychopathy, and sociopathy), I believe a brief introduction to what personality disorder is, and all it entails would be helpful to lay a solid foundation. Mind you, the purpose of this chapter is to help refine your understanding of what narcissism is by cutting out the many uneducated perceptions you have had in the past.

So, What Is Personality Disorder?

To understand what personality disorder is, one must first understand what personality is. Thankfully, previous chapters in this book have been dedicated to explaining how personality is formed, which is more or less the interaction between a child's temperament and the environment, the temperament of a child being determined by its DNA. The nature of personality is intrinsically fluid, which means a healthy personality can easily blend in with the several social structures of society with as little friction as possible. A healthy personality will easily understand any society it finds itself in, the individuals within it, and the written and unwritten rules of engagement. All of this is done with a level of personal aspiration balanced with empathy, meaning someone with a healthy personality can easily cope wherever it is put without causing any form of damage, deliberately (consistently).

However, personality disorder is a superset of several disorders characterized by rigidity in personality, making it hard to understand social norms, empathy, and normal human interaction, leading to acting in ways that put both itself and others in harm's way (Grohol, 2015).

From the first definition, you notice that personality disorder is considered a "class," meaning it is seen as a group of several disorders. These disorders are numbered to ten and grouped into three different clusters: Cluster A, Cluster B, and Cluster C.

Since this book is specifically written to deal with Narcissistic Disorder, I will not bore you with all ten personality disorders. However, we will focus on Cluster B.

The Cluster B Personality Disorders. According to Steliana (2015) and backed by the DSM-5, Cluster B includes four disorders; antisocial, borderline, histronic, and narcissistic. People that fall within Cluster B are usually dramatic, emotional, and erratic.

Furthermore, you would notice that antisocial (also called sociopathy or antisocial personality disorders) and narcissism both fall under Cluster B! In essence, both disorders share certain traits. However, they are different.

Differences Between Sociopathy and Narcissism

- A patient with ASPD does not care about the law, whereas a narcissist is fully aware of the law and the consequences of breaking it.

- A sociopath does not care about people's opinion of them, while a narcissist's ego is built upon comparison with others.

- A sociopath is prone to violence, while a narcissist isn't primarily prone to being violent.

- A sociopath acts in ways to hurt others (being violent, wicked, and damaging) without being provoked. They do not need any motivation beyond being bored. A narcissist only lashes out if his ego is bruised.

- Although both sociopaths and narcissists are lacking in empathy, the latter is due to a high level of self-centeredness. This means a narcissist, at least, can still understand how his actions might be affecting others.

- The sociopath cares deeply about himself and, by extension, can project perverted love to others. A psychopath does not care about others and could also care less about himself. A psychopath will put himself in danger without a thought.

- A sociopath does not have a sense of self-depreciation or shame. A narcissist fights shame, self-rejection, self-depreciation, and self-hate, all of which they cover up with nasty, maladaptive habits.

Similarities Between Sociopathy and Narcissism

- Both can be very charming to their intended victims.

- The covert narcissist and the sociopath often find it hard to maintain the activities of daily life and may be forced to take up substance abuse.

- Both have a higher chance of being incarcerated; however, with ASPD, it is higher, with reports stating that 40 percent of prisoners have ASPD. Also, repeat offenders are higher in patients with ASPD.

Psychopathy

In my research of personality disorders, the biggest revelation I came across was the fact that psychopathy is not a clinically diagnosed personality disorder. This is even though it is considered the worst type of personality disorder, characterized by extreme violence, rage, and madness!

Arguably, there are more movies centered on psychopaths than any other personality disorder! Psychopathy is synonymous with ASPD. This means most of the traits considered to be psychopathic are all listed under sociopathy.

Chapter Six

Understanding Why You Are Drawn To Narcissists

How often have you heard women say, "I always end up with the wrong man." Perhaps you have made the same statement several times. So, why do we always end up with certain kinds of men or women? Is there an invisible mark written on our foreheads that only narcissistic people can see? Are we destined for a life of emotional abuse?

This chapter will seek to explain all of these.

The Burden of Responsibility

I must establish certain facts before you delve deep into this chapter. You must understand that the term "victim" is not used derogatorily. If you have been traumatized by a narcissist or are currently in an abusive relationship with one, you are strong. Your assumed weakness tells a tale of how strong you can be. The burden of responsibility for all the abuse, gaslighting, and emotional trauma you have been through or are going through falls on your narcissist and not you.

Secondly, I need you to review this chapter with an open mind. We all have areas in our lives and mindsets that often make us prey to bad people. There is absolutely nothing wrong with that. In a safe and ideal world, we would all love with our eyes closed and be accepted. Much like Eden, we all would be naked, yet none ashamed. But this is not an ideal world. As illustrated in Chapter 1, the fact that people are primed to hurt others deliberately is a fact of life. The purpose of this book is to equip you with as many mental weapons as possible to wade off or manage these predators, men and women who are set in their ways and would rather cling to the dark than light. So, approach this chapter with as much openness as possible so you can understand yourself better.

The Story of Echo

The legend of Narcissus is popular. The man loved his reflection so much that he died staring at it! However, a lesser-known character in the myth is also essential. Her name is Echo.

Echo was a nymph cursed to repeat the last words of people or sounds that objects made (the sense of humor of mythical gods is indeed disturbing). She, unfortunately, crossed paths with Narcissus, and like everybody who crosses paths with this beautiful man, she immediately fell head-over-heels in love with him. However, unlike others, Narcissus did give her attention. But, remember, Echo can only repeat the last words spoken to her. So, for everything Narcissus would say, poor Echo would simply repeat the last words. No one knows why, but after a while, Narcissus rejects her as he always does. He leaves Echo brokenhearted. Alone and sorrowful for not being able to have her love reciprocated by Narcissus, she dies. Narcissus' rejection of Echo angered the gods, who sent a spirit to deceive him into falling in love with his reflection.

Again, this story has several renditions, but this sums it up.

The dynamics of the relationship between Narcissus and Echo reveal to us the dynamics of the relationship between a narcissist and his victim.

Victims of narcissists are perfectly matched for a narcissist. The self-obsessed narcissist meets with someone who amplifies what he thinks of himself. Echo speaks back the last words of whatever Narcissus says. Echo, much like you, is made not because of any fault of hers to soothe the ego of Narcissus, an ego that cannot be settled. Narcissus can never be satisfied. Even though Echo provides all the worship and attention within her power, Narcissus eventually denies her. Narcissus will get bored one day and move on with another, or probably die alone. This is the saddest reality of most abusive relationships: the victim comes to realize, after many years of doing his or her best to keep her abuser happy, that there was never a hope of a happily ever after. Let us now demystify the curse of Echo in the next section.

The Curse of Echo

You were introduced to schemas in Chapter 2. At this stage, I believe you can diagnose (not as a professional) someone with NSD or high narcissistic traits, as well as probably guess what their childhood must have been like. But that is just one side of the coin. The other side is using your understanding of schema to demystify why you always end up a victim. The difference between a narcissist and his victim isn't usually much.

The very curse placed on Narcissus is similar to the curse on Echo. They both die alone, with Narcissus staring at his reflection and Echo with a broken heart from being rejected despite doing all she could to get Narcissus. The underlying cause of death in both cases is unfulfilled desire.

The Mind of a Victim

Most of us have one or a combination of schemas. The more healthy individuals are those who have learned to resolve childhood issues. They have mastered mindfulness, the ability to assess themselves, people, and situations in the present within reasonable contexts without unnecessarily internalizing things. Remember, I explained thoroughly that every child is born with a unique temperament: happy, shy, timid, warm, open, curious, etc. This temperament is dependent on the DNA of each child. I also stated that temperament can change. However, the most important lesson from Chapter 2, based on Young's schema therapy, is that what a child will become is an intersection of their personality and environment. The 18 schemas depend largely on the interaction between a child's temperament and the environment. However, what will determine if a child would be narcissistic or be a victim is the child's reaction to his schema when he grows up! Hence, the difference between a narcissist and his victim is how they have chosen to react to their schema!

As we explore this further, I must remind you again that schemas are more present in the subconscious region of the mind. This means they are there, but you are oblivious to them. Also, your reaction towards each or a combination of your schema is often subconscious. In essence, both you and the narcissist are not in control of your actions. You both are like computers, programmed to react to actions based on programming installed in you.

The Schemas of a Victim

According to Behary (2008), there are eight primary schemas unique to a victim. These schemas are listed below, followed immediately by how a victim reacts and a story to help make the point!

Self Sacrifice

This is the fundamental belief that you must sacrifice your human right to please others.

Eric grew up a middle child to two amazing parents. His father was an out-of-town lawyer. The mother is a high school teacher. At an early age, Eric found himself in quite a quandary. His elder brother was brought up to be responsible, more or less to be able to help with basic household chores. Eric, however, is a year older than his younger brother, who was around and has always had their parents, neighbors, and practically everybody gush over him.

Unfortunately, Eric always felt like he didn't exist. His elder brother seemed way too mature for his age and commanded the respect of both their parents, while his younger brother sucked all the attention to himself because of his charm. As early as Eric could remember, he was always forced to let go of toys to his younger brother. Because of how close they were in age, they liked the same thing. But his parents expected him to sacrifice things all the time. There was nothing he could do to make his parents see that he felt cheated. But he soon realized that every time he let go of his comic book, his favorite toy, or something significant to him, he got the applause of his parents. Even though short-lived, he enjoyed his parents' attention in those moments. He subconsciously built the belief that he had to sacrifice to be loved.

Eric's Reaction: Eric is now a 35-year-old Christian. He has a history of dating women who use him! His last relationship lasted about six months. He was madly in love with one of the ladies in the Choir, a narcissist. She was a covert narcissist (of course, Eric is not equipped to see through her). It wasn't as though she was beautiful or had the best voice, but she was influential in the Choir thanks to her willingness to take on the duties most people wouldn't do in church. But people closer to her are more aware of her judgmental attitude. Her best statement was, "Nobody is righteous, moral, nor sacrificial enough like Jesus, of course, except her." She ensured everybody knew how long she had to go hungry for a beggar on the street. Eric fell in love with her because he thought he saw a kindred spirit. Unfortunately, she was insatiable. Eric sacrificed time, money, and resources to be the best man for her, but she was never satisfied. He would try to out-give her in offerings and handling more church projects, but it was never enough. The only reason they broke up was because she had to move. Eric offered to leave with her to keep the relationship, but she refused. She explained that she cared too much for the Church for Eric to leave. She would rather sacrifice their relationship on the altar than have him move with her.
But despite this, Eric firmly believes, much like Echo, that he didn't do enough to keep her.

Eric's Curse: He is cursed to react to demanding people by sacrificing himself to gain their love and attention.

Subjugation

This is the belief that your needs and wants aren't valid. This is almost similar to self-sacrifice. But, where self-sacrifice doesn't invalidate needs and wants but sacrifices it to please others, subjugation invalidates needs and wants. A subjugate feels shame when their own needs are met.

Shelly is a product of a single mum. She never met her dad. Her mum was a waitress when she'd had her and remained so for most of her adult life. Her early days would involve several men coming in and out of her and her mum's life! For as long as Shelly could remember, her mother rarely expressed herself! It wasn't that she had nothing to speak about, but she felt ashamed doing so. Over and over, Shelly overheard most of the men her mum dated telling her she didn't deserve them, asking her how many men would gladly date a single mother, taking on the responsibility of being a father to a girl who wasn't theirs. She rarely saw her mum ask for anything, and when some of these men physically assaulted her, she took the beating quietly. The only time she tried standing up for her mum against a man, she was shouted down by her mum. The man looked at both of them with disgust and said, "You both don't deserve to be happy."

At 23 years old, Shelly is currently locked up in a relationship with a guy she met a year ago. At first, he was kind and seemed interested in her. A few months into the relationship, he starts to treat her with a level of scorn she was well too familiar with. He makes all the decisions in the relationship. He would listen to what she wants but then go ahead and do that which pleases him. But Shelly never complains. Yet, no matter how much she submits to his supreme leadership, he always finds a way to attack her. Today, as Shelly stares out the window of his condo, she doesn't know what else to do to please her man. But she would try to keep the relationship going one day at a time.

Shelly's curse: Shelly is cursed never to express who she is because she is ashamed of herself. So, she acts based on the demands of those around her.

Abandonment

This is a belief that a loved one would abandon you. You believe nobody would ever remain faithful to you.

Dapson has no memory of his mum. All he knew was that he was barely a year old when she left him and his dad. This was a story his grandmother consistently told him. He always wondered why his mum would leave. Was he a bad kid? Did she hate him? What did he do wrong? Answers never came. He, his dad, and his grandma stayed together. He was pretty close with his dad. He remembers several trips he took with his dad out of town. He remembers sitting up way after bedtime, waiting for his dad to return home from work at night. He also remembers vividly the day his dad told him about a trip he would have to take. His dad never came back. They got the news that he was involved in an accident. But he only got to know about this after so many years. His grandma wanted to save his fragile heart from pain. It wasn't quite long after that his grandma died, having spent months in the hospital. She died from cancer. It was on the week he graduated high school. After the burial, he left his country home for good.

Dapson's Reaction: Today, he is a successful videographer. Everyone knows Dapson is a good person. But he can be a little bit clingy. He would do anything to have his team around him. There was no escaping his firm grip. Sadly, this also has made him a victim to several exes. His current girlfriend is rumored to be unfaithful. But Dapson doesn't believe the rumor, even though it is true. He defends her brutally. He tells people she is good to him and is always there for him. And he is correct. She is always with him, not because she loves him, but because she knows Dapson has a shot at working one day with a big production company. It is an opportunity she needs to capitalize on for her acting career. Some say Dapson is fully aware that his girlfriend is evil; if only Dapson could be less clingy, he could see for himself.

Dapson's Curse: Dapson is cursed to do anything he can to hold on to anyone who shows him any form of kindness and love.

Emotional Inhibition

This is the belief that showing emotion is a weakness and makes you vulnerable.

Tim stood in front of his dad, shaking in terror. His mum stood behind him quietly, looking unfazed. His hand trembled violently behind his back as he held tears back. "WHO BROKE THE WINDOW?" his father barked the question at him for the second time. Tim mustered his courage and spoke firmly, "I did." There was a brief silence, but deep. With each second of silence, the tears he held back pushed through, making way a drop at a time. He saw the disappointment in his father's eyes! He knew what was coming next, a chide for his crying. His father's mantra resounded in his ears: "A real man does not cry. Only weak people and human beings show emotions in the face of war. Tim never saw his mum cry. He never saw his dad express any real feelings towards anybody. When Dad's friend stole all of his money, Daddy said nothing. When Daddy met with his friend and the friend was cussing Daddy out, Dad sat quietly with Mum beside him. When the man returned some of the money he stole, Daddy thanked him. This was how Mum and Dad treated every opposition.

Tim's Reaction: Tim is quiet and reserved. He figured out early in life how to deal with bullies: "Do not respond." Several times, he has been shoved and attacked, yet he never gave off any sign of fear or worry. "I will never let them see me cry," he whispers to himself. Although at night, he would soak his pillow in tears, away from the eyes of many, away from the observant eyes of his father, the same eyes that have never stopped looking at him since the day he broke a window. Many think he is weak and tolerant of the many abuses he has been a victim of, especially at his workplace. His boss, a maniac, would ridicule him before the entire staff. His head of department would pass down grunt work to him. Yet Tim doesn't complain. He quietly takes it all.

Tim's Curse: Tim is cursed to never express himself. He is a moving target for practically all types of narcissists.

Reading the stories above, you will notice that some victims share a couple of schemas. This is common. The human mind is complex, and it is tedious to unravel the several reasons why we act in certain ways under given conditions. This explains why the road to healing isn't from point A to point B but rather several roads intertwined.

Below are the four major combinations of schemas for a victim.

- Mistrust and Subjugation
- Defectiveness and Unrelenting Standards
- Abandonment and Emotional
- Deprivation and Self-Sacrifice

How The Brain Works During A Threat

With the previous section, you should have seen the correlation between what you are going through or have gone through and the several stories shared. You would also most likely be in denial, as you probably have never actively followed your mind process to see why you act the way you do around your narcissist. Everything, as mentioned earlier, happens in your subconscious. You rarely remember your mum who left you when you were a kid when your husband says he has to go on a trip. But your body remembers, and at that moment, it mimics precisely how you felt years ago. The information (data of the feeling) is stored in your brain and will activate in certain conditions. This is why you act like you do but do not know why. Below is a more scientific way to view how your mind works.

Dan Siegel explains in "The Low Road" the workings of the brain when it senses a threat succinctly. According to him, when our brain perceives a threat, it sometimes shuts down the prefrontal cortex, which is the part of the brain responsible for logic and thoughtful reasoning. When shut off, we lose the ability to interpret what we see or hear logically (Siegel 2001, 2007; Siegel and Hartzell 2004). When you are before your narcissist, put in a scary condition, one that is similar to one in your childhood, you lose your sense of logic, and your subconscious takes over. Your reactions in the moment come from your subconscious, which is programmed to act a certain way.

Chapter Seven

Healing Yourself, The Art Of Mindfulness

In the previous chapter, we examined how a victim's mind works. Specifically, we were able to match the schemas of a victim to its narcissist. We established that the same schema that turns a child into a narcissist is the same that prepares another one to be a lifelong victim of narcissism. In this chapter, we will be going a step further. The goal here is to demystify and help you understand yourself more to heal. At the end of this chapter, you will learn how to:
- Identify your schema
- Identify what triggers you
- Take control of yourself via mindfulness

Identifying Your Schemas

The logical thing to do when a problem must be solved is to ask, "Why?" The answers to "why" would often lead to the root of the issue. So, why are you still in a relationship with your narcissist? Why does your boss get to your last nerves, yet you find yourself consistently loyal to him? Why can't you just let go?

It isn't strange that you have provided answers to these questions. Some popular answers include:
- Because you love them
- Because you need them
- Because they are important to you

Yet these answers have not quite brought the comfort you

need. Because the fact is:
- You can love them and not be triggered by them
- You can need them and not have your personality assassinated by them
- They can be important to you, and the relationship can still be meaningful

In essence, the responses you have rationaled are not correct. The correct answer is, "You are still with them because you are programmed to." Your schema matches their schema. You do not know why you are still in the relationship because a different part of you, the subconscious, controls your actions. If you desire freedom, you must, therefore, identify your schemas. So go through the last chapter and note down the different schemas discussed. Mind you, you can have more than one schema thanks to the complex way our brains store data.

By doing the exercise below, you will recognize your schema or schemas. Note that this exercise is not given as a replacement for proper therapy.

Take time to answer the following questions to identify your schema.

Did you grow up in a family where you were consistently made to feel ashamed or guilty for wanting things for yourself?

If yes, then your schema is self-sacrifice.

Were you bullied into silence as a kid? Were you forced to keep quiet whenever you wanted to make a point? Do you fundamentally believe that for peace to reign, you would rather keep your opinion to yourself?

If yes, your schema is subjugation.

Do you fear being abandoned by those you love? Did you lose any parents at a young age? Are you adopted? Did any of your parents leave and never come back?

If yes, then your schema is abandonment.

Were you made to feel shame because of something unique to you? Perhaps you were ashamed of how you spoke or expressed yourself. Do you blame your uniqueness as a reason why you were treated with scorn as a kid?

If yes, then your schema is defectiveness.

Do you believe it is a thing of honor to be able to take a lot of insult and abuse without showing emotions? Are you stoic? Did your parents demand you never to show weakness or extreme emotions when in pain?

If yes, then your schema is emotional deprivation.

Did you have an emotionally absent parent? Were you given much attention as a child, or were you neglected? Do you fundamentally believe no one would show you love?

If yes, then your schema is emotional deprivation.

Were you abused as a child, physically, sexually, or mentally, and you learned to take it in without protesting? Do you believe your abuser would stop if you allowed him to do what he wanted?

If yes, then your schema is mistrust.

Do you have very high standards for yourself in terms of relationships? Do you believe you must strive to be perfect at all times? When things don't work out, do you feel like it is because you didn't do your best?

If yes, then your schema is unrelenting standards.

As you go through the above exercise, make sure to note down your schemas.

The next step is for you to identify your triggers. In the previous chapters, we established the following:
- Schema exists in the subconscious
- Schemas are activated by today's events that are similar to childhood events
- The difference between a narcissist and a victim is how they react to their schemas

You must understand the above points, as it will help you identify your triggers.

Identifying Your Triggers

The best way to identify your triggers is via observation. So, what you want to do is to begin journaling your experience henceforth, especially moments you feel your narcissist is at his element or when you feel attacked.

Key things to journal include:

The context of an incident: This means the location, what led to that particular moment, what was said, etc.

Perhaps you decide to go on a dinner date with him. You both have agreed on a date. But the day comes, and he uncharacteristically gets home late. Instead of apologizing, he begins to rant about how he had to leave things unfinished in the office, how important work is to him, and a list of other nonsense.

Some details you might want to jot down would include:
Whose idea was the date?
How much effort have you put in to prepare for the said date?
His attitude before the day.
Your expectation for the date.

Your narcissist reactions: Next, you need to jot down how your narcissist acts. In the above scenario, you can jot down:
He acts as though the idea of the date has caused him some damage.
He threatened never to accept any future proposition for a date ever again.
He storms into the room and refuses to speak to me again.

Your feelings: At this stage, you want to jot down everything you felt as you watch your narcissist act.
Did you feel threatened he might never speak to you again?
Did you feel shame for attempting to enjoy a nice time with your husband?
Did you keep quiet and let him rant, knowing fully well that your silence would encourage him to stay silent or act?
Did you want to speak out and remind him you both agreed on the date and it was his responsibility to check his calendar, as it is his responsibility to call and cancel when something came up?

The more you can journal your feelings, the better.

Your reaction to your feelings: Jot down your eventual reaction. It could be:
- You kept quiet.
- You apologized to him and promised never to come up with stupid ideas again.
- You wanted to speak but feared being yelled at, so you complained quietly.

The more information you have, the better.

Analyzing Yourself

Your trigger: This is everything that happened before your narcissist's reactions. You have lived this moment over and over in your childhood. All the times you happily informed your dad about your next game, recital, etc.—you looked forward to this day and couldn't wait to show your dad how amazing you were. But he never showed up.

However, today, it is not your dad but your husband. Immediately, he was a few minutes late for the date, and it activated your schema, which is your fundamental belief.

Your feelings: What you felt when your narcissist didn't show up when he came back home and began to act strange is a total of your schema.

You felt stupid for thinking you could have a nice time.
You felt you should have called him hourly to remind him; you could have done more, and you think it is your fault he came late.

You know it is his fault, but you fear speaking out might make him madder.
You worry because of this event, he might never speak to you.

Go through the list of common schemas to victims, and note your schema.

Your reaction: Your reaction to the above incident reveals exactly why your narcissist still has power over you. You keep quiet either because you fear being shouted at or you are stoic: It gives the narcissist more control. He feels he has conquered you.
You promise to do better and be a better wife; it gives the communal narcissist a feeling of righteous dominance. He has shown you your flaws.
You make up for the missed date by showering your husband with accolades, gifts, and attention. You give the overt narcissist a sense of superiority, feeding his perverse sense of entitlement.

Changing Yourself via Mindfulness

If you journal your experience over a period, you would by now be certain of your schemas, their several triggers, and how you react to them. With this information, what you want to do next is heal yourself.

First and foremost, your schemas are maladaptive. They are faulty mindsets. Secondly, you must remember that your reaction to the trigger of your schema is automatic. It comes from a place beyond your control. This is why you feel helpless in your relationship. Everything you do is somewhat out of your control, more or less like you are being remote-controlled.

To therefore take control of your life back, you must be able to:
- Face your fear and accept it.
- Understand your programmed reaction towards it.
- Feed yourself new information on how to react in similar situations.

To achieve the above, you must practice mindfulness. So, what is mindfulness?

Mindfulness is the art of being conscious and aware of one's present moment, to notice and observe one's feelings and bodily sensations. With mindfulness, you can capture sad moments that birthed your schemas. Next, you will allow the dark emotions these moments conjure up to fill you. Your objective will not be to judge or block these emotions. Next, you will observe your reactions to these feelings, physically and mentally. The goal is to be an observer, to watch your past life unfold before your eyes. Finally, you will educate your mind on how to react to these emotions using words of affirmation properly.

Note that the process illustrated above can take time to master. I would not want you to rush into things. So, I will introduce easy mindfulness practices. Do these every day, and you will immediately begin to observe how grounded you have become, how you can understand yourself in situations, how your body responds to events, and what your innate desires are. In doing this, you gain control of yourself and can make decisions more from a calm mind and consciousness than from the turmoil of an emotional wave.

Practice1.

1. Sit down comfortably on a mat or the floor and focus on your sense of breathing. Just breathe; you don't have to do deep breathing or try to count your breaths. Just breathe and focus on how it's happening. Feel it coming through your nose, your throat, or even in the chest and diaphragm.

2. Feel your breaths. By doing so, you're kept grounded, and you get to the point where you see that breathing is amazing and keeps you alive.

3. Bring your attention back to your breathing whenever your mind wanders off. Don't criticize yourself, though. Just tell yourself that you're breathing.

You can practice mindfulness in the everyday activities of your life. Remember that the goal is to be present within the moment, to observe your interaction with the external world, and to be aware of everything happening inside and outside you.

- Eating: Take time to observe every meal. Take in the aroma and watch how you respond to it. Do you feel like taking a bite immediately? Be aware. Taste the meal, and notice the taste, each palate. What comes to your mind? Does it bring back any memories? Does your tummy rumble for more? Do this as often as you can.

- Touching: What are your favorite clothes? Hold it in your hands and feel its texture. Let every thread run through the skin and note how it feels. How does your skin react to it? What color is the cloth? What about the clothes that draw your attention the most? Find out and observe your attraction towards it. Do not judge how you feel; do not question how you feel. You are strictly an onlooker at that moment!

- Music: What is your best song at the moment? Listen to it and give yourself to it. Is it danceable? If yes, then dance. Observe how your legs move. Are you a bad dancer? Then, watch with amusement as your brain struggles with controlling your body to the song's rhythm. Take note of how you feel in every note. Study the emotions that well up as the words from the lyrics hit you.

- Nature: Take a stroll on the beach. Notice how calm you feel. What else do you feel as airbrushes pass you? Are you taken back to a time in your past when you were still a child? Take in the feeling of the beach sand in between your toes. Watch and observe everything.

- Communicating: When you next converse with someone, observe who you're talking to. Are they smiling or frowning? Open your entire self to them and monitor your reaction to the words they speak. Look into their eyes and watch your energy match or repel them. Take note of the tightness in your gut as you react to the hurtful things they say. But don't judge.

Mindfulness is a powerful state of being. Now, to apply it to your schemas, do the following:

1. Make a sitting posture with your feet planted firmly on the floor, or sit cross-legged on a mat. You can also sleep straight, facing up.
2. Create an anchor point for your mind by taking note of your breathing. Your mind will wander, but bring it back

to the moment.
3. Go back in your mind to a painful childhood experience. If your schema is subjugation, you can go back to a time when your parents shouted you down as you tried to explain why you wouldn't want to change schools.
4. Allow your mind to relive the experience. Focus on as much of the memory as you can. Observe how you feel. Is it shame, anger, fear, or anxiety? Whatever you may feel, let it take over you.
5. Observe your reaction to these feelings. Observe how you immediately lower your head in fear. Observe your knee going weak. Feel the knot in your tummy as you keep quiet for fear of your father coming at you in anger.
6. Take in everything. Remember, you are bold. Remember, this is just a moment in time, and it is no longer real.
7. Now, take charge of your reaction by communicating truths to your mind at that moment. Tell yourself the truth: "I will speak my truth even in the face of hostility. Nobody can force their opinion down my throat without my allowing it. Peace can reign in an honest and open argument about issues."

Speak as much truth to yourself.

You have done well. Now, repeat the entire process once every day. The more you do it, the stronger you get at controlling your reactions.

You will begin to observe changes in your communication with your narcissist. You will be more present when he begins to scream at you. You have lived this moment over and over and over. You'll notice that your old habit of forced submission will try to kick in. But you are in control now. You might do nothing or say nothing for a while, but unlike before, you are fully aware of everything happening in and around you. As you grow stronger, you notice you can say your truth respectfully. You might wait for him to finish ranting, and hours while he sits quietly feeling like a king, you walk up to him and say,

"I did not want to offend you further while you made your points a few hours ago. But I see now that you are calm. What I have to say is……" Then, conclude with," I am not imposing my thoughts on you, as I believe in your ability to make amazing decisions. However, I would like you to think about all I have said. And when you are willing to have a more healthy conversation with me, let me know."

Chapter Eight
How To Manage Yourself

How do you feel?

Do not skip the question above. At this stage, you have a robust understanding of why you find yourself drawn to your narcissist or why you are currently stuck in a relationship with one. You understand your schemas, and you have a sense of what triggers them. Most importantly, you are more equipped to act in the moment, taking control of your body rather than giving in to your brain's natural tendencies. In essence, you are on your way to becoming a more healthy individual.

Kudos to you; you should be proud of yourself. I wouldn't be surprised if you struggle sometimes or even give in, but remember: "Baby steps."

The Single Factor That Determines if a Narcissist Will Change - Leverage

No man is capable of changing another. Today, many perish under the sea for attempting to change someone they love. Ironically, who they assume needs saving is sipping a mojito on a beach in the Bahamas. The point I am making here is unless someone is willing to change, you will be wasting your time. Drag them through a million couple's counseling or book them a billion appointments with the best shrinks in the world. If they have no intention of changing, nothing will come out of your efforts. Accept this fact, and you will know peace. Also, depending on how manipulative your narcissist is, he will charm your pants off and can act all changed to have you back away from him/her to keep you entangled in the relationship. I must tell you this before explaining what leverage means. Leverage is an incident so traumatic that it drives a narcissist to look at himself instead of his reflection, causing him to see how ugly he/she is and motivating him/her to want to change. It could be a major illness, the loss of someone they cared about, or an elongated suffering of some sort.

Managing Your Narcissist

- Know Your Narcissist
- Identify His Trigger
- What Not To Do
- The Art of Communication
- Run For Dear Life

Know Your Narcissist

The first step to managing your narcissist is to identify the type he/she is. If you read the entire book to this point, then without a doubt, you should be able to know the kind of narcissist you are dealing with.

1. Does he project a sense of grandiosity? Does he act, believe, and think he is better than others? Is he charismatic?

If yes, then you are dealing with an overt narcissist.

2. Does he have a sense of superiority but isn't

charismatic? Does he criticize and attack people unnecessarily? Does he sometimes play the victim in situations where he is clearly at fault? Does he have a high sense of entitlement? Does he desire to be showered with praise even in simple tasks? Does he resort to gaslighting?

If yes, then you are dealing with a covert narcissist.

   3. Is your narcissist unnecessarily competitive? Is he the type that can sabotage a competitor just to get ahead? Does he hate losing arguments with people? Is he the type that tries to force his ideas down other's throats?

If yes, then you are dealing with an antagonist narcissist.

   4. Is your narcissist extremely self-righteous? Does he constantly boast about all the amazing things he has done for others and you? Is he prone to maligning the personality of others just to feel good about himself? Is he deeply critical of people's motives and considers himself the standard for right living?

If yes, you are dealing with a communal narcissist.

   5. Is your narcissist self-centered, shows no sense of empathy towards people, is sometimes prone to violent fits, and is completely incapable of socializing without others? Do you feel constantly threatened by his presence or think he may harm you?

If yes, you are dealing with a malignant narcissist.

Armed with the knowledge of what type of narcissist you are

dealing with, you can manage your narcissist.

Most Likely Triggers of Your Narcissist

To identify the triggers of your narcissist, you might have to journal your experience with him. The goal is to be able to map out common scenarios that make him act his worst.

Below are a few triggers common to each type of narcissist.

Triggers of the covert narcissist
- When you question or criticize them
- When they are being compared to others, especially those who are ahead of them
- Ignoring them
- Disrespecting them
- Highlighting your success before them
- Practically any situation that reveals their weakness or highlights the strength of others

Triggers for the overt narcissist
- Refusing to acknowledge them
- Criticizing their accomplishments
- Challenging their authority
- Attempting to outshine them
- Showing unnecessary weakness (They prey on the weak)
- Challenging their abilities
- Ridiculing them
- Associating yourself with people they consider inferior

Triggers for the communal narcissist
- Not living up to their standard

- Ignoring their deeds
- Acting against their moral code
- Associating yourself with other people they consider "unworthy"
- Calling them out on their hypocrisy
- Demanding they show accountability

Triggers for the antagonistic narcissist
- Competing against them
- Not showing dedication to their cause
- Associating with those they consider enemies
- Not acknowledging their victories
- Criticizing their weaknesses

Note that you do not need to have the intention of doing any of the things mentioned above for your narcissist to be triggered. However, if the scenario looks like it, your narcissist will react!

Communicating With Your Narcissist

Properly equipped with all the knowledge you have of your narcissist, one of the fundamental skills you must develop is the ability to converse with him. With proper communication, you can:
- De-escalate issues when they arise
- Shield yourself from frequent attacks

There are five basic rules to guide your communication with your narcissist.

Remain Calm

Irrespective of the situation, remain calm. Your narcissist is screaming at the top of his voice, reminding you of how you are nothing without him. Be calm. Your narcissist has locked himself away emotionally as a means to torture you. Remain calm - he will eventually come around. Your narcissist is passing derogatory statements camouflaged as jokes at you in public. Remain calm. Whatever you do, the last thing you want is to give him or her the pleasure of triggering you.

Allay Their Fear/ Doubt/ Pain

One of the first things you want to do when you decide to speak is to firmly assure them you are not an enemy. This can go in many ways. With an overt narcissist, you can start with:

"I understand you have worked hard to get to where you are."

"I acknowledge the amount of work you have put in to be where you are today."

Assure Them Your Action or Inaction Was Not Meant as an Attack

This is very simple and direct, and the goal here is to help them see that even though you didn't mean to hurt them, you fully understand why they might be acting up.

Let them see that You Are Ready to Communicate if They Are

Assure the narcissist you are open to discussing whatever it is they are agitated about and are willing to set the record straight. Promise to be as transparent as ever.

Let them see that their action Hurts You and Has Consequences

Let your narcissist understand that his actions were wrong and that you do not appreciate being spoken to or treated in that way. The purpose of this is to set boundaries.

Obviously, these rules are not written in stone, but more importantly, they cannot be applied to every scenario. However, they are elements you should master.

Run For Dear Life

In most cases, I advise victims to leave a relationship with a narcissist unless they are mature and healed enough to manage such a relationship. If said narcissist is a parent or sibling, then I advise you to create boundaries. However, in cases where you are being physically abused, you are dealing with a malignant narcissist, or your narcissist is relentless in hurting you, then run for dear life. Never remain in a relationship where abuse has become normal.

Remember, a narcissist can be violent, but he isn't violent because he is a narcissist. Violence is a symptom of a worse personality disorder. If you are dating or have someone like this in your life, do the right thing and report it to the police.

Ensure you get a restraining order. Do everything possible to have them stay away from you. Do not be tempted to tame that Lion. You will always be a bad day away from being eaten alive!

What Not To Do

There are so many who have engaged their narcissist using the wrong methods, and by doing so, only made things worse. Below are a few things you shouldn't do.

Do Not Apologize

Never take responsibility for a crime you did not commit. You can love your partner to the ends of the world but never take responsibility for what they have become. You had nothing to do with their schemas. Never be guilt-tripped into thinking they are what they are because of something you did. They were already messed up before you met them.

Do Not Attack

Consider that your narcissist is what he is today by negative reinforcement. Attempting to attack a narcissist would only make the situation worse. Your narcissist might keep quiet, retreat, or seemingly surrender to your attack, and it may seem as though you have won, but you have not. A fundamental ingredient when it comes to change is accepting who we are. Unfortunately, a narcissist's biggest fear is to confront that little child in himself that needs healing. The brief moment of victory for you is seething for him/her to plot an act of revenge. You would by now notice this circle in your relationship. You keep quiet and allow the narcissist to continue his damage, and he continues. You counterattack, and he comes back worse, more manipulative, and dangerous.

Do Not Try To Change Him

This is one of the biggest mistakes victims make in every relationship. They almost always assume that their abuser is with them because they are special and, as such, have a degree of control over the abuser. However, this isn't really the case. A lion will pursue its meal with vigor and passion. It doesn't do this because the antelope means nothing more than food. You thinking you can change a narcissist is like an antelope that thinks it can change the nature of a lion. This book is not written with a promise that you can change a narcissist; it is written so you can understand the nature of a narcissist; it is for your own nature, helping you to heal and exit or be able to manage yourself if you decide to remain in that relationship.

Chapter Nine
Becoming A Healthy Narcissist

I expect that you are on a journey to healing completely from your narcissist. I also believe you have taken the bold step to cut your narcissist off or are becoming an expert at managing your relationship with him. It is only fitting that I leave you with a parting gift. And that is an understanding of what you should aim for - which is to be a healthy narcissist. You should be familiar with it by now, as I have used it several times in this book.

So, what really *is* healthy narcissism?
According to Psychcentral (2023), the term healthy narcissism is not official. The closest we have to it is primary narcissism, which is an adaptive narcissistic trait unique to children. However healthy narcissism has come to mean many things, but it boils down to traits that each of us must possess to live a healthy and fulfilling life, one that balances how we view ourselves with how we view others. Healthy narcissism ensures we can express ourselves positively without exploiting others and instead become a source of motivation.

I was able to come up with seven key elements I believe we all need to become healthy narcissists, and these are discussed below.

Self-love

Self-love is the foundation of being a healthy narcissist.

Do you love yourself?

We live in a world where no one escapes the lemons life throws. We all have issues from our childhood. Even those blessed among us with amazing parents still had to deal with damaged teachers and hurting students at school. Nobody is completely free from abuse. But, to triumph, we all must begin making lemonades from our lemons. What I mean is no matter how life has spun your web, you have no choice but to rise and take responsibility for yourself. That responsibility starts with you loving yourself. That responsibility begins with you pouring as much positivity into yourself as you need until you are free from the shackles of your schemas and maladaptive narcissistic traits. The biggest problem you will face in this journey, as most who have begun, is "understanding what love truly means."

So, what is love? In simple terms, love is everything positive. It encompasses all that leads to a positive state of mind, body, and soul. Love is more than a feeling. And even though its existence can be measured—it is infinite. This is why the practice of self-love must become a habit in itself. You must be deliberate with it. If you sense you are running out of self-love, retreat and take up some more. So, how do you practice self-love?

- Accept yourself: How can you accept others if you are not comfortable in your skin? Acceptance, first and foremost, isn't about validating yourself. It is about being factual with what you know about yourself and realizing that, at that moment, it is the best version of who you are. So, you accept the bad and the good with

as little judgment as possible. This can be achieved via practicing mindfulness.
- Build Yourself: After acceptance, you need to begin a journey of building yourself. And the best tools for making one's self are words. I am a big believer in positive affirmations. Daily, speak words of encouragement, hope, joy, and love to yourself. You do not have to believe them at first, but with many words come the ability to believe. You can transform the negative in you into positive by speaking the right words to yourself daily.
- Gift Yourself: Many struggle with doing good to others because they have not learned to do good to themselves. I strongly believe that the first person deserving of our good deeds is ourselves. Treat yourself right first, and you will understand why others need to be treated right.
- Forgive yourself daily: This is the focal point of self-love. You will mess up sometimes and can't do anything about it. The faster you are at forgiving yourself for missteps, the better.

Build Healthy Relationships

None of us can choose the family we are born into, but we can choose the family we want to be with. The foundation of a healthy relationship is mutual development. What I mean is that you must decide to surround yourself with people willing to love you as much as you are willing to love them. It is the law of reciprocity. Treat all humans with decency, but keep only those who love you as much as you love them around you. Stay away from negative spaces. If you cannot help it, call out negative habits as much as possible through proper communication. Set boundaries to ward off people bent on pulling you into their self-made abyss.

Be Purpose Driven

Choose to live for a cause greater than yourself and play your part. We all must leave behind a legacy. Your cause does not have to be a popular one. It only has to be something true to you. You can decide to dedicate a part of yourself to helping lost puppies.

Take Pride in Accomplishments

Always be the first to pat yourself on the back when you achieve something. Make it a practice to tell yourself, "I am proud of you," before anyone does. This kills the need to be boastful. But, if there are eager ears and smiling faces interested in hearing firsthand about what you have done, then do tell. Enjoy the moment, and be sure to give flowers to all those who helped you along the way, then step down when the ovation is loudest to do more amazing things.

Develop Empathy

Empathy is a learned trait. So, if you find yourself unable to understand what others are going through, choose to live a day in their shoes. What most narcissists lack is empathy, as they are blinded to the feelings of others. So, develop empathy. One of the best ways to build empathy is to travel a lot. Taking yourself away from your comfort zone and immersing yourself in the environment of others will help broaden your emotional, cultural, and moral perspective enough for you to accept others.

Conclusion

If you made it this far in this book, I am proud of you. Without a doubt, I know you have been fully equipped with all the information you need. The good news is you are a step ahead of your narcissist. You can:
- Identify a narcissist a mile away
- Diagnose, to a degree of accuracy, the schema, trigger, and reaction of a narcissist
- Identify your own schemas, triggers, and reactions
- Manage your emotions and actions around a narcissist using the art of mindfulness
- Plot your way out of a toxic relationship with a narcissist

Mind you, always celebrate the little wins in your journey to freedom. But, more importantly, never forget that I believe in you.

REFERENCES

1. American Psychiatric Association (1994) Diagnostic and Statistical Manual of Mental Disorders, Fourth Edition. Washington, DC, American Psychiatric Association.
2. American Psychiatric Association (2022) DSM-5-TR Classification (1st ed.). Amer Psychiatric Pub Inc.
3. Anastasopoulos, Dimitris. (2007). The narcissism of depression or the depression of narcissism and adolescence. Journal of Child Psychotherapy. 33. 345-362. 10.1080/00754170701667197.
4. Behary, W. T. (2008). Disarming the narcissist, Surviving and thriving with the self absorbed. New Harbinger Publications, Inc.
5. Ellis, H. (1898). Auto-eroticism: A psychological study. Alienist and Neurologist, 19: 260-299.
6. Freud, S. (1905,1953). Three essays on the theory of sexuality. In J. Strachey (Ed.), The standard edition of the complete psychological works of Sigmund Freud (Vol. 7, p.135-243). Hogarth Press Ltd: London.
7. Freud, S. (1914/1991). On narcissism: An introduction. In J. Sandler, E. Person, & P. Fonagy (Eds.) Freud's "On Narcissism: An Introduction" Yale University Press, New Haven.
8. Grohol, J.M. (2015). Personality Disorders. PsychCentral.com.
9. Horney, K. (1939,1966) New ways in psychoanalysis. W.H. Norton & Company: New York.
10. Jones, E. (1913,1951) Essays in applied psychoanalysis, Vol II: Essays in folklore, anthropology, and religion. Hogarth Press Ltd: London.

11. Kernberg, O. (1975). Borderline conditions and pathological narcissism. New York: Jason Aronson.
12. Man, J. (2004). Genghis Khan: Life, death, and resurrection(2nd ed.). St. Martin's Griffin.
13. National Library of Medicine. Does a narcissism epidemic exist in modern western societies? Comparing narcissism and self-esteem in East and West Germany. (2018, January 24). https://www.ncbi.nlm.nih.gov/pmc/articles/PMC5783345/#:~:text=Narcissism%20is%20increasing%20in%20modern,1992%20in%20adolescents%20%5B2%5D
14. Reich, W. (1933,1972). Character Analysis, 3rd ed. New York: Farrar, Straus, & Giroux, Inc.
15. Rizeanu, Steliana. (2015). PERSONALITY DISORDERS. Romanian Journal of Experimental Applied Psychology. 6. 60-65. 10.15303/rjeap.2015.v6i4a.
16. Stanford Institute for Economic Policy Research. (n.d.). *Surviving a school shooting: Impacts on the mental health, education, and earnings of American youth.* https://siepr.stanford.edu/publications/health/surviving-school-shooting-impacts-mental-health-education-and-earnings-american
17. Wälder, R. (1925) The Psychoses: Their Mechanisms and Accessibility to Influence, International Journal of Psycho-Analysis, 6, 259-281.
18. Young, Jeffrey E., Janet S. Klosko, and Marjorie E. Weishaar. 2006. Schema Therapy: A Practitioner's Guide. New York: Guilford Press.

About the Author

With a Bachelor of Science degree in business, and a self-taught education in human behavior, Alexi has always had the uncanny ability to read and understand people. Working in a sales career sparked an interest in learning more about narcissistic personality disorder after dealing with a narcissistic boss and multiple narcissistic co-workers.

Fueled by Alexi's wealth of experience dealing with different types of people he debuted his first non-fiction novel "The Narcissist's Lifestyle: How To Live And Deal With Narcissistic Personalities" a book that unravels narcissistic personality disorder. This is a book written with simplicity, and the information is supported with revealing stories.